God Is Holy

Sermon Series by

Pastor Peter Balciunas

Transcribed and Annotated by

Alison Bitney

DEDICATION

My journey in this life has been sculpted by our Holy Triune Creator for which I owe my life. Thank you God the Father, God the Son, and God the Holy Spirit. I thank my wife of 23 years for her gentle loving support through the most difficult storms. Patricia, I love you 'mostest'. I couldn't do what I do without your spiritual insight and discernment. I give thanks for my family who continue to surprise me with selfless acts of service and love. Thank you Chandler and Laurel Balciunas. I thank the one who had prophetic vision to see this book through, from conception to end with superb literary finesse. Thank you Alison Bitney for your help and friendship. Thank you Andrea Bitney for your friendship as well as helping your mom, Alison, in this project with divine direction. Thank you Brian Bitney for being an anchor for your family and prayer pillar for our church. Grayson, thank you in advance for piloting God's ministry around the world (this is prophetic vision...just saying). Thank you Rob David for your friendship and detailed additions with biblical expertise. Thank you Awake Christian Church family for your unwavering love, commitment and generous support. I also thank the church elders: Brian Kirkpatrick and wife Monica, Rob David and wife Ann, Scott Hillman and wife Adrianne, Dr. Don Richards and wife Donna for your prayers, support, apostolic leadership for almost 10 years, working together and making Jesus the most famous individual in the lives of our local community and the world. I would like to thank our sister churches in India, Shalem Full Gospel Ministries led by Pastor Sharon Raju Pekala and wife Mahima Grace for their service and prayer covering. God is Holy!

CONTENTS

ACKNOWLEDGMENTS

Thanks to Andrea Bitney, Megan Peterson, and Roben David for their contributions in editing and content.

INTRODUCTION

The Spirit and the Word call us to holiness. God is calling us to raise His standard of holiness. Unpacking this attribute of God is a daunting and humbling task. How do we explain the holiness of a spiritual being who is so far above our human understanding? How do we explain an almost indescribable attribute of an intangible eternal being?

In February, 2016 I began teaching a 7 week series on the holiness of God at my home church. As I went through the series, I watched my congregation transform and experience things they had never experienced before. In my 30 years of ministry, I have never encountered God's Holiness to the degree that I experienced at this time. Our hunger for God has increased. Our reverence of God is deeper. Our love for each other has been noticeable with actions and community. We are seeing deliverance from demonic spirits, healings, miracles, and prodigals returning to God. Our worship of Him has changed. Going to church is no longer about what we can get from God. We no longer seek Him for what we need, although, our needs are being met. We now seek Him because of who He is and what He desires of us......Worship, Reverence, Honor, and Thanksgiving.

> "Who is like You among the gods, O Lord?
> Who is like You, majestic in holiness,
> Awesome in praises, working wonders?"
> Exodus 15:11 (NAS)

The answer is, no one is like Him. No other spiritual being is like Him and more importantly, we cannot compare Him to ourselves. **He is Not like us**. God's attributes are not human. We cannot think of God in human context.

The Church has humanized God in such a way that the carriers of His Standard have fallen into the sin of familiarity. We have forgotten who He is and who we are in light of His holiness. The standard which He designed for His people has been lowered to such a degree that we no longer realize we serve the infinitely perfect God. The Banner that The Church once held is tattered and trampled by humanism, frailty, sickness, poverty, and the like.

The Church is out of alignment with God. Its reflection looks more like the world than it does Him. Pastors all over the country talk about God, however, the fruit of their preaching has created an immature body of believers who are not yet prepared to become the Bride of Christ.

Our programs, our departments, our many ministries, our exhaustive ritual and oration has not produced a fitting companion for our Lord. What is missing? Where is the confirmation of all these good works? If God is present in them, there should be lasting signs of His Presence. Where are the miracles, healings, deliverances, the fortitude, sanctity

2

of marriage and sacrifice? What are the signs that follow the believer today? Exhaustion, burn-out, defeat, fear, weariness, and families torn apart. Something is out of alignment.

The Church has forgotten who God is, and how we are to approach such a Holy, Omnipotent being. The scriptures are full of His glory, love, and grace. We have concentrated on these attributes because they provide a positive message. **Now is the time to look fully at Him, (if you dare).** Facing a Holy, Almighty God demands change. It is imperative for the Church to awaken! He calls us to repentance so that we will be a vibrant, holy reflection of His image and purpose. He wants to empower us for the work that lays ahead in these very last days... the end of this age.

.

CHAPTER 1
"BUT THOU ART HOLY"
(Psalm 22:3)

As a human in a fallen world, it is easy to forget who God is, especially since the contemporary church has humanized God (Father, Son, and Holy Spirit). Today's church leaders have reinvented God, making the idea of God more palatable to the people. This only serves to meet their own understanding and human need. The God that many preach is more like Santa Claus or an Iron Fist.

God is Holy. Even His name is holy. YHWY is His name and it is very old. At some point in time, the Israelites began to believe that His name was so holy, that normal mortals better not pronounce it. They substituted "Adonai", the word for "Lord". (abarim-publications)

> "You shall not misuse the name of the
> LORD your God, for the Lord will not hold
> anyone guiltless who misuses his name"
> Exodus 20:7 (NIV)

This scripture is one of the Ten Commandments that God

gave to Moses on Mount Sinai. After the Israelites left Egypt they came to the Desert of Sinai and camped there, where Moses climbed the mount to meet with God. In chapter 19 we read:

> "This is what you are to say to descendants of Jacob and what you are to tell the people of Israel; 'You yourselves have seen what I did to Egypt, and how I carried you on eagles' wings and brought you to myself. Now if you obey me fully and keep my covenant, then out of all nations you will be my treasured possession. Although the whole earth is mine, you will be for me a kingdom of priests and a holy nation.'" Exodus 19:3-6 (NIV)

After hearing God's directive through Moses, the people proclaimed that they would do EVERYTHING the Lord had said. Moses brought back the response of the people to God and God said:

> "Go to the people and consecrate them today and tomorrow. Have them wash their clothes and be ready on the third day, because on that day the Lord will come down on Mount Sanai in the sight of all the people. Put limits for the people around the mountain and tell them, Be careful that you do not approach the mountain or touch the foot of it. Whoever touches the mountain is to be put to death'"
> Exodus 19:10-12 (NIV)

God commanded the people to prepare themselves for His

presence because they were unclean and sinful in His eyes. This preparation was not for His benefit, but for their own protection, so that they would not die in His presence. He is so holy that when He descended onto the mountain, the ground became consecrated. All 7,497 feet made Holy by the presence of God.

On the third day the consecrated people followed Moses to the base of the mountain! As God descended, thunder, lightning, smoke, and fire encompassed Mount Sanai. The entire mountain trembled violently as Moses ascended. It was in the presence of all these fearful wonders that God gave the Ten Commandments, the law for the people to live by.

Keep in mind that God is the same yesterday, today and forever. (Hebrews 13:8) HE HAS NOT CHANGED! It is impossible for Him to change. God is perfection itself, He is light, and there is no darkness in Him.

We say that we want to know God, but if you were Moses on that day, would you be able to stand in the presence of God's Awful Holiness? No! Without protection we would die.

While meditating on the Holiness of God, I could not help but take account of my own relationship with Him, being convicted and concerned about myself and the church as a whole. I believe, even after 30 years of ministry, that I have not treated God with the appropriate respect that knowing Him demands. I feel unworthy to speak on this because I am far from holy. However, I am drawn, called to **come up** to meet God on the Mountain. I feel a need to prepare myself in order to meet this Incredible, Indescribable, Eternal, and

Almighty being.

Thank God that Jesus has given us access to the Father. Without the cleansing and sanctification of the Blood of Christ, we would die in His presence. His blood covering is absolutely necessary for any type of relationship with the Father. To enter Heaven's gate, the blood of Christ must be present. It is the only payment for admission, but once inside, we have a responsibility to God that the Church has been neglecting to teach.

An unbalanced hail-fire and brimstone teaching took over the Church many years ago. The teaching that started in holiness turned into legalism and brutality. The pendulum in this time has swung the complete opposite direction. Now, a cheap grace that removes our responsibility to the Kingdom of God is being preached, which perpetuates a lack of authentic fear and respect for God This teaching, taken to extreme, negates God's overwhelming Holiness in the minds of His people.

Current Church messages are concentrated on self-betterment rather than on knowing who God is. These messages will not conform us to His image. We can't be satisfied with knowing only about Him. Truly knowing Him changes us. He wants us to come up the mountain. He wants us to see Him for who He really is.

Christians today ask how they can use God in some formula to manipulate Him to act on their behalf or help in their circumstance. They come to Him, unprepared, ignorant of His holiness. They see Him relegated to a person who looks and acts like them, an acquaintance who might be able to give them what they desire. (This sounds similar to the way some people view government). Churches provide a feel-good atmosphere that superimposes surrogate encounters with God to help hold the congregation's attention. Church goers are easily bored and will hop from one church to the next. They are seekers of a better formula. They are users and askers of God. They do NOT know HIM. They know that Jesus, their big brother (with a high five slap) laid his life down for them....They feel just that important. But they do NOT know the God on Mount Sinai. They do not know the God who created all things. They do not know HIM.

If they did know Him, the Church of Jesus Christ would look different. They would posture themselves differently when coming to Him. They would come to Him, not with hands held out begging His favors, but with hands uplifted, worshipping the one that gives them breath... The one that upholds everything with His word...The one who will remove this world and the heavens like removing a garment.

In a quest for wisdom, we must seek Totality teaching. This presents us with a "both/and" scenario, in that we must BOTH understand our sin AND recognize our Savior.

> "The Fear of the Lord is the beginning of wisdom; and the knowledge of the Holy One is understanding. For through wisdom thy days will be many, and years added to your life." Proverbs 9:10-11 (NIV)

Fear of the Lord and the knowledge of the holy, and the Holy One will bring an increase of days to you.

He is majestic. He is Holy. He deserves (and demands)

better than what the church has done so far. He desires more from us. A true holiness encounter with God will leave us stripped of everything we thought was valuable. We will be left gazing at His Holiness, offering only one thing....humble worship that comes from a place of love, honor, respect, and awesome holy reverence. This type of encounter will compel us to treat God differently and treat each other with more honor and care.

> "Behold, He puts no trust in his saints; yes, the heavens are not clean in his sight. How much more abominable and filthy is man, which drinks up iniquity like water." Job 15: 15-16 (AKJV)

In Job 15:15 Eliphaz the Temanite, a friend of Job's, indicts God's people when he says that God puts no trust in His saints. Although this is merely an opinion from Job's friend, we must realize that for most of us and for most of our actions, it is a true accusation. Only by God's grace and mercy are we able to become more than this. God is perfect. We are NOT. The Blood of Jesus covers our imperfections. Without this covering, that He alone provided, we are not able to go into His presence.

We imagine God as a proud papa, looking over His creation...The sun is shining on us and He is proud of His children and their attempts at life. In our imagination He is just waiting to care for us, heal our hurts, give us our first car, to cheer us on in our endeavors. We see Him thrilled at the end when we are handed the participation trophy.

This is how God sees us:

9

"How then can man be justified with God?
Or how can he be clean that is born of a
woman? Behold even the moon, and it shines
not; yea, the stars are not pure in His sight.
How much less man, that is a worm? And the
son of man, which is a worm?" Job 25: 4-6
(KJ2000)

Ouch!

In this scripture the son of man is not a reference to Jesus. It
references to a person. A worm that has a baby is a worm.

Why is this important for us to understand? This is how God
views man. We must come down from our pedestal and
realize how holy God is. We are closer to a worm than we
are to God.

It is impossible to intellectually grasp the infinitude of God
and not consider that we are mere worms. Like a grizzly bear
walking with an ant. The ant must wonder what significance
it has for the bear. The ant can't do anything for the bear, yet
the bear desires the companionship of the ant. We can offer
God nothing that He could not do by Himself.

He has always had all power. He has always existed. He has
always been as holy as He is now.

While presenting this message to my church on Sunday
morning, after reading this scripture, a woman and her twenty
one year old daughter looked at each other in some kind of
recognition and began to cry. Her mother interrupted the
service and said that I had to hear what had happened to her
daughter. I knew that God was doing something. The young

woman shared that she had seen an open vision during that week. She told her parents about the vision and although she did not understand all of what God was trying to tell her, she continued to seek God for the interpretation. This young woman had just recently come to God. She is a statistics major at a university. She works with her professor in scientific research of DNA. I say this to tell you that I consider her to be reputable, but new in the Lord and has not been around the things of the Spirit during her lifetime. She is sincere and I believed every word. The vision was this:

> While the young woman was laying in her bed, before falling asleep, and with her eyes wide open, a ball about a foot in diameter appeared above her bed near the ceiling fan in her bedroom. She said the ball was made of bloody worms. They were all entangled, and some of the worms were falling onto her bed and blood was dripping onto her bed. They looked diseased and disgusting. She said that the vision was about 7 seconds long. She immediately related it to sin, and how God views the world. A heavy intercession came over her and she wept and prayed for the people of the world. She was so saddened by their state that she experienced a physical ache.

She and her mother were crying because it was such a confirmation that God did give her the vision and wanted her to understand it. My message that morning was part of the explanation.

I was amazed at the timing and the fact that God was confirming her vision in this message. I was convinced that God was speaking to us, His people, about Holiness and showing us that we are far from the condition he desires for us. We are sick with sin, diseased, and we are not walking in His holiness. We are no help to the world in this state.

CHAPTER 2
HOLY, HOLY, HOLY IS THE LORD OF HOSTS
Isaiah 6:3

It is impossible to intellectually grasp the infinite existence of God. He has always existed. He has always known all things and been all powerful. He has always been holy. Every attribute of God is in complete concert. We have no real concept of infinity or holiness. Everything that we are and everything that we do pales in comparison to His Holiness. God has always had all power. He has always been completely perfect and thoroughly holy. The only way to begin to understand his holiness is through the blood covering of Christ.

For the Old Testament saints, the two key components of blood sacrifice were the condition or attitude of the heart, and the perfection of the sacrifice. In order for the sacrifice to be acceptable, it had to be without blemish and given in an attitude of sincere devotion. This is the manner we, as believers, are to approach our Most Holy God. At the time of our salvation we acknowledge Christ's blood sacrifice and are then covered so that we may approach the Father. Jesus was (and is) the perfect sacrifice. When we come to Him sincerely, we receive forgiveness of sin (realizing that in ourselves, we could never come before a perfect God). As new believers, we don't yet understand the depth of His perfection and holiness. However, time spent with Him in prayer, instruction, and worship opens our hearts to deeper understanding….understanding the holy. It is futile to come before the Lord in any other attitude than sincerity. If we come to Him any other way, He will not commune with us. He cannot look upon imperfection. In fact, it is repulsive in His sight. In the book of Isaiah we see that God is not pleased with insincere offerings.

> "What are your multiplied sacrifices to me?
> says the Lord. **I have had enough** of burnt
> offerings of rams and the fat of fed cattle. I
> do not delight in the blood of bulls. Or of
> lambs or goats." Isaiah 1:11 (ESV)

Isaiah served as a prophet of God in the time of Uzziah, the King of Judah. He was called as prophet during the last decade of King Uzziah's reign. Isaiah continued to prophesy unto the people of God through four kings until his death. Isaiah's main purpose was to declare God's judgement on the sin of Judah, Israel, and the surrounding nations. He prophesied in hopes of turning God's people away from disobedience, and ultimately restoring the promise of redemption, the advent of the Messiah, and the salvation of the nations.

> "In the year that King Uzziah died, I saw
> also the Lord sitting on the throne, high and
> lifted up, and His train filled the temple.

Above it stood seraphim; each one had six wings: with two he covered his face, with two he covered his feet, and with two he did fly. And one cried to another and said: "Holy, holy, holy is the Lord of hosts; the whole earth is full of His glory!" Isaiah 6: 1-3 (KJ2000)

Isaiah's ministry began at the end of King Uzziah's reign (although, many believe that Uzziah's son, Jotham, was already serving as leader). To understand the spiritual environment of that time, we must look at the life and service of Uzziah.

Uzziah became king of Judah at 16 years of age. He ruled 52 years. Although his father, Amaziah was still living, the people of Judah made Uzziah king instead of his father. Amaziah had been a mighty leader of armies and defeated the Edomites, but he ended up in idolatry of the Edomite gods.

Uzziah's reign was militarily beneficial and prosperous. In the beginning of his reign he followed God and listened to the prophet Zechariah, and was faithful to God.....Until he wasn't faithful. In speaking about Uzziah, Jeremiah writes:

"And he did what was right in the sight of the Lord, according to all that his father Amaziah had done...." 2 Kings 15:3 (KJ2000)

"...except that the high places were not removed; the people still sacrificed and burned incense on the high places" 2 Kings 15:4 (KJ2000)

15

The high places are a reference to the altars of idolatry and worship of other gods.

In the beginning of his reign, Uzziah was blessed. The people of God were blessed. Uzziah was resourceful, inventive, and knowledgeable. He led successful military campaigns against God's enemies. His armies dispossessed the Philistines, Ammonites, Gurbaal, and Moabites. He restored the country's fortifications, he enjoyed notoriety, and his fame was spoken of in Egypt (2 Chronicles 26: 8-14).

His reign proceeded well until he forgot that God had allowed his success. In pride, Uzziah perceived his accomplishments to be of his own glory and ability. The fact that he did not destroy the high places, along with the presence of his massive ego, led him to destruction.

> "But when he was strong his heart was lifted up, to his destruction, for he transgressed against the Lord his God by entering the temple of the Lord to burn incense upon the alter of incense." 2 Chronicles 26:16 (KJ2000)

The appointed priests of the temple warned him and attempted to stop him. They told him that he was dishonoring the Lord. By disregarding God's standard and design, Uzziah dishonored God. He thought that he was sanctified enough to perform the priestly duties. He exalted himself and argued with the high priest. He entered the Holy Place in the Temple, despite the priest's objections, and as he approached the Golden alter of Incense, leprosy broke out on his forehead. The priests immediately ushered him out. He remained a leper until the day of his death and lived in isolation while his son Jotham reigned in his place. Jotham took heed and obeyed God.

Coming to God with a wrong attitude or self-exaltation will cost you. Disregarding God's design or instruction will cost you. You and your offering will be rejected by him.

Our heart is the key to our worship of the Most Holy God. His holiness could not accept the insurrection of Uzziah and will not accept ours. God has not changed. Is it not a wonder that the people of God today are diseased, prideful, ineffective, and out of order?

> "In the year that King Uzziah died, I saw also the Lord sitting on the throne, high and lifted up, and His train filled the temple. Above it stood seraphim; each one had six wings: with two he covered his feet, and with two he covered his face, with tow he covered his feet, and with two he flew. And one cried to another and said: 'Holy, holy, holy is the Lord of hosts; the whole earth is full of His glory!'" Isaiah 6:1-3 (KJ2000)

The first five books of Isaiah calls the people to repentance. He points out their sin and declares their punishment. Before we can see God as He is, we must acknowledge our sin and repent. The Uzziah personality must die in all of us...and when it does, we will see God's Majesty just as Isaiah did.

For us to see God, repentance is only the beginning. To understand the knowledge of His holiness, the sincere, heart-felt, and authentic worship of Him is required. As we come before Him in this posture, He transforms us little by little.

"And the posts of the door were shaken at
the voice of him who cried, and the house
was filled with smoke. Then I said: Woe is
me, for I am undone; because I am a man of
unclean lips, and I dwell in the midst of a
people of unclean lips; For my eyes have seen
the King, The Lord of hosts." Isaiah 6:4-5
(KJ2000)

When we come to Him, with a repentant heart, He is not
silent. He comes to us as the smoke. He cannot display
himself to us without killing us. As He protects us from His
holiness, He comes to us by means that we can understand.
Smoke, mist, fire, light.....all of which we can see in this
dimension and live. Being in His presence causes us to fall
on our face in fear and reverence. In this place of
communion with Him, we realize something that goes
beyond our initial salvation. We are acutely aware that we
are unclean in comparison to Him.

We are aware that our garments are dingy and our speech is
filthy and inadequate. The world in which we live is just as
corrupt as we are. Because no flesh can stand in His
presence, our fleshly characteristics are revealed. His
Holiness demands change. Just when you think you've got it
all together, like Uzziah you are reminded of your place. God
is supreme and His design is the only pattern that is
acceptable.

If we follow this pattern, He will NEVER leave us undone!

"Then flew one of the seraphim unto me,
having a live coal in his hand, which he had

18

taken with the tongs from the altar: And he laid it on my mouth and said: 'Lo, this has touched your lips; and your iniquity is taken away, and your sin purged.'" Isaiah 6:6 (KJ2000)

His Spirit of holiness has the power to change us.

"If we say that we have no sin, we deceive ourselves, and the truth is not in us. If we confess our sins, He is faithful and just to forgive us our sins and to cleanse us from all unrighteousness." 1 John 1:8-9 (KJV)

Uzziah is no different from us today. We are prideful, arrogant, and full of all kinds of disgusting attributes and motivations. We don't listen to God's prophets. We are stubborn and think that we know best. We seek position. We covet fame, and possessions. We want God to bless us without the sacrifice of obedience and respect.

CHAPTER 3
BE YE HOLY FOR I AM HOLY
1Peter 1: 15-16

As we contemplate God's attributes, we can't help but see our lack. However, as we sincerely worship Him in spirit, truth, honesty and repentance His holiness has the power to change us.

> "This is the message which we have heard
> from Him and declare to you, that God is
> light and in Him is no darkness at all. If we
> claim to have fellowship with him, and walk in
> darkness, we lie and do not live out the truth.
> But if we walk in the light, we have fellowship
> with one another, and the blood of Jesus
> Christ His Son cleanses us from all sin." 1
> John 1:5 (NIV)

There are no words as to whether Uzziah repented…He lived in isolation. Man was not meant for isolation. Man was meant for fellowship with both God and man. Until his death, Uzziah was without fellowship. **If we do not see true**

fellowship in the church today, it is due to sin.

When we walk in repentance and holiness, we are not separated from God or man. John goes on in Chapter 2 to say that because Jesus is the sacrifice for our sin, we can know him; we can walk in His commandments; we can be perfected; we can abide in Him; we can love the brethren; we can overcome our enemies, the flesh, the lust of the eyes, and the pride of life. Verse 28 says that at His coming, we will not be ashamed but have confidence. He goes on to speak of walking in righteousness.

> "And every man that has this hope in Him purifies himself just as He is pure."   1John 3:3 (KJV)

In the light of God's infinitude, like the ant, it is inevitable that we feel small and insignificant. This is an accurate understanding of us as compared to God. All power and control is in His hands and when we realize that He is the Grizzly, then we will understand that there is no point in questioning His will and design.

When we add holiness to the infinitude of God, we see that we are not only powerless, but that we are vile. This should magnify the need for Christ in our lives. When we sense our own vileness and do not repent, then, we become ashamed. When we are convicted of our sin, it is not God's intention for us to dwell in shame. He wants to cleanse us, and work holiness through us. But if we do not repent, our shame locks us into a revolving pattern of sin.

The contemporary church doesn't preach conviction for this very reason. The pastors don't want to cause the parishioners to feel vile. When people are convicted of sin with no ability to recognize how to become clean, they feel ashamed. These parishioners either leave the church or remain in their seats week after week, stuck wandering in the wilderness rather than being led into the promise land. The church has not provided a path that leads beyond shame.

In order to avoid internal conflict, messages are being
preached that reduce the standard of God.
This type of preaching (or should I say placation) attempts to
keep church seats filled week after
week. These messages sedate and seduce parishioners. A spirt of slumber has permeated the body of Christ. Parishioners are relegated to bill payers! The so-called men of God teach that man is good. That God's grace can be trampled and that repentance from sin is passé. They don't want others to feel bad about themselves. They do not consider God's Holiness.

The Bride of Christ is to be spotless, without blemish, which emulates the type of sacrifice that was brought to God in the Old Testament. However, the Church is fallen; morally, physically, intellectually, and spiritually. Humanism has crept into the church and has sought to dilute God's Word, therefore, making it impossible for the mission of the Church to be fulfilled. When we are born, we enter a fallen world, and in every capacity, we are fallen beings. We learn impurity from the cradle and there is no escaping it. The humanistic/demonic message being heard today is that man is intrinsically good. Psychology has replaced spiritual truth. Multistep programs, mantras, and the joining a 'church club' has not helped to conform the Bride into His Image. These dangerous doctrines reduce the standard of God, lowering the bar so that God's people feel better about themselves. These messages have caused the people of God to detour from experiencing the very thing that will cure them.

People seek positive messages, feel-good sermons, and affirmation of their dead works. They seek like-minded people who confirm their own misguided feelings. They feel bruised or hurt if the minister speaks the truth in love, because they do not want correction. Like Uzziah, their arrogance brings them to the house of God, unprepared, unsanctified, unwilling to obey God's design, and unwilling to repent. The priests at least tried to stop Uzziah.....not so today. Ministers, with open arms, tell them that they are fine. The parishioners feel good about themselves for even going to church. When they step out of the church, that good feeling is lost....and so are they.

Mankind is Far from God....two ends of the spectrum. Our whitest white is grey in comparison to Him. You will not go to heaven because of **your** goodness. **He** alone provided the way for eternal salvation. You will not walk holy and spotless by anything that **you** have accomplished. **He** will purify you as you come to Him in reverence, humility, repentance, worship, hungering and thirsting for Him. God will not be manipulated or impressed by your goodness. Your positive attributes are as filthy rags to Him. The Fear of the Lord, conviction, repentance, and confession are the things by which you are called to continue. By practicing these same things, you will be conformed to His image.

God is not like us. He is not human. We must get away from seeing him as human. Humanity is fallen. Jesus, the son of the Father, had to lower himself to be clothed in humanity. The scripture says that humanity was created lower than the angels. God, the Son, condescended to humanity so that fallen humanity could relate to Him. Jesus did not sin. He was spotless. His blood and DNA were pure. Therefore, He was qualified to be offered up as the final blood sacrifice for our sin. With that pure blood He bought our freedom from eternal condemnation. Believing in Christ is not the end of the journey for God's people. Salvation ("sozo" in Greek) is a verb, an action word. Its meaning includes ongoing restoration, healing, and deliverance (past, present, and future). Through Christ, we begin the journey of sanctification, (we were saved), and continue into purification (we are being saved) and ultimately we will be presented as His Bride, completely sanctified, set apart for Him...a spotless Bride for the One who gave His life for us (we will be saved). Through Christ, we were Justified by His substitutionary death for our sins (we were saved), we begin the journey of Sanctification being "set apart" and continuing in holiness as we surrender to His Lordship (we are saved), and ultimately we will be Glorified when we are presented as His Bride, an eternal spotless Bride for the One who gave His life for us (we will be saved).

The Church says that 'The world needs God'. The same is true for the contemporary church. It's true for every believer past, present, and future. Needing God's intervention is ongoing. Learning about His character, attributes, plans, and design is a life-long endeavor. We must see Him as He is. A Supernatural Spiritual Being who must lower Himself so that we can encounter Him.

CHAPTER 4
I AM THAT I AM
Exodus 3: 14

Authentic revival always begins with an authentic encounter with the Holiness of God. Once we encounter His Holiness, all of our earthly intentions fade and we realize that we are nothing in comparison to WHO HE IS. He is The GREAT I AM THAT I AM. As God restores His truth, signs of confirmation of that truth will follow.

When God made the covenant with Abraham He swore on Himself because there was not anything higher. He equates His Holiness with Himself. Again, He speaks of this truth when making covenant with David:

> "Once I have sworn by My Holiness; I will not lie to David." Psalm 89:35 (KJ2000)

In the time of Uzziah's reign over Judah, Jeroboam reigned over the Northern tribes of Israel, the prophet Amos prophesied judgment against Israel. They heard God swear by His Holiness.

"The Sovereign Lord has sworn by His holiness…" Amos 4:2 (NIV)

The fact that He places His Holiness as high as Himself shows the gravity that He places on holiness. When we contemplate this, we are confronted with our deficiency.

The Church realizes, at least in a small way, that for us to travel from 'point A' (apostasy) to 'point B' (becoming the Bride), there must come a tremendous move of God. For His Church to realign with His purpose and design, we must re-evaluate WHO God is:

> He is Deity, Eternal, and Self Existent. He is Infinite. He has existed forever. There is no beginning or ending to Him. He is not limited as humans are. There is no one higher than Him.

> He is Holy. There is no impurity within Him. He is perfect in every way. He is Light and there is no darkness in Him at all. In Him, there is no sin.

> He is Love. He alone is Good, Merciful, Gracious, and Just.

> He is All-Powerful and Self-sufficient. He is Sovereign. He has the final word.

> He is All-Knowing. He has All Wisdom. He never lacks Foresight. He knows all things. He knows the end from the beginning.

He is present everywhere. "There is nowhere that His presence and His sovereignty is not felt."

He is Unchanging. He is Impassable (not overwhelmed, weakened or stifled with emotion). He is determined and does not waiver.

He is Jealous over His creation. He oversees our atonement. He is the Author and Finisher of our faith.

Once we see Him for who He is, we will change. For us to be able to see Him as He is, we must be like Him.

> "Beloved, we are God's children now, and what we will be has not yet appeared; but we know that when He appears we shall be like Him, because we shall see Him as He is. And everyone who thus hopes in Him purifies himself as He is pure." 1John 3:2-3 (ESV)

When people have a true encounter with God, they are transformed, just as Moses was changed, even physically, when he came down from meeting with God. Preaching hell-fire and brimstone won't change us. Preaching hyper-grace won't change us. Both of these positions are wrong posturing before Him.

God is calling us up to a higher place. His Spirit is drawing us. The Word of the Lord has gone forth, is going forth, and will go forth to direct us. His people are destined to become like Him. Knowing God is essential for this change to take place. Although we will be like Him, He remains supreme.

The Church has been operating in severe error. Motivated by wants and needs, His people have come to church, spent time in "prayer", sang the songs, and acted in the "correct" manner, but they continue to be unchanged, unholy, fearful, diseased, and distracted. If the motivations for coming to God are founded in wants and needs, there will be no contentment. When God tarries with their answer, healing, or desire, His people become weary. They feel loss, rejection from God. They become offended at God. They stop seeking Him. They fall away. They expect the church to meet their needs and when the organization does not, they leave.

If, however, we came to God in humility, reverence, and worship (which is His design), we would not be disappointed. The truth is that God designed the Tabernacle for Himself! His motive was to live with a people who would Worship HIM. Our wants and needs are secondary to communion, fellowship, and intimacy with God. The contemporary church has devised smoke and mirrors to keep people in the seats. In doing so, they have relegated the worship of God to singing, programs, outreaches, entertainment, etc. Instead of going to God with true worship, we go to Him with a list of requirements, desires, needs, and hurts.

My hope is that you understand God's Holiness and that you pursue Him for who He is, and not what you can get from Him. If you have the former, He will meet your needs, and give you the desires of your heart. He will hear you. He will answer. You will not be disappointed.

Honoring God is the key. We see people in other religions honoring their gods. How much more should we honor the One True God? He wants nothing separating you from Him. Not your cares, nor needs, nor hurts....nothing that would take your heart away from true worship of HIM. You can't come to God while having some hidden agenda. Nothing is hidden from Him. Every motivation of your heart is known to Him. Any motivation beyond true worship of Him is sin. You must not let your humanity and human need stand in the way of honoring and worshipping Him.

Some people go to church to "network" with others. In so doing, they hope to add to their business, company, ministry, election, and success. Self-promotion in the place of worship is much like the moneychangers in the temple. Jesus was disgusted. He was moved to righteous anger. When Jesus saw how His Father's house had been utilized for self-gain, He cleaned out the place and reprimanded them.

> "It is written, he said to them, "My house will be called a house of prayer, but you have turned it into a den of robbers."" Matthew 21:13 (NIV)

Who were they robbing? God and His people. This is serious business. Later in Matthew he tells the people to give to Cesar what belongs to him....AND to give to God what is God's. Worship belongs to our Holy God! The temple was built for God's people to come to worship their Holy God. That is the motivational design for gathering in the church. When we come to Him with any other motivation than complete worship and adoration, we are robbing Him. If we are leading the people to come to Him in any other way, we are robbing them of an authentic encounter with God which could very well save their lives. Sin leads to death.

When, however, we focus on His many attributes, realizing

29

that He holds the breath that we breathe, we will treat Him differently. We will come into His place of worship crying **"Holy, holy, holy is the Lord of Hosts."**

 The seraphim covered themselves with their wings, and they cried one to another, "Holy, holy, holy is the Lord of Hosts." When we pray for God's kingdom to be manifest on the earth, we pray that we will mirror what is happening in heaven. This is the type of honor and worship that is happening in heaven. No creature or saint comes into His presence without a covering. They all fall on their faces and cry out "Holy, holy, holy..."

Heavenly creatures know how to address God. But His children on the earth do not. The unbalanced teaching from pulpits today is not helping us understand Him. Coming to the throne of God boldly does not mean in arrogance or in familiarity with Him. We can be assured that because of Christ, we have entrance into the Holy place to worship and commune with our Holy Father. However, the Church must come into alignment with His standard. God will not condescend to ours. **Lowering the bar of God so that people feel comfortable is not the mission of the Church**. We are to be standard bearers. Upholding and conveying the standard to the people. We must put Him first. We must repent. We must lay our agenda's down. This is the challenge for today.

What will happen when we begin to see His Holiness? We will see Him as He is. Then we will become like Him.

Americans do not expect their leaders to be honest, trustworthy, holy or truthful. The standard in politics and business has been lowered so much that those that are trying to be upstanding are ridiculed. This upside down philosophy has permeated the church today as we see men of God in all types of sin. This is not God's design. The Church should mirror Christ. We should look much different from the world. We should be the example of holiness in our cities, nations, and the world. **The world cannot broker holiness. Holiness is something the Church is solely responsible for.** The standard of holiness must be picked up, dusted off, and flown high so that those that are dying in their sin can recognize and receive the help that God alone can give. This seems too daunting of a task, however, the church is set apart for holiness and the world should be able to see it clearly upon us.

True holiness is seen as an irritant to the world. Maybe this is why the church does not preach it. Perhaps they want as little confrontation with the world as possible. As long as there is no contention, the church-goers can sit, listen to good music and positive messages. Like children, they can be babysat and entertained. They won't need to feel bad about themselves or hear hard things. Church-goers can feel relatively good about their Sunday experience. They can pat themselves on the back for going, and leave the building, congratulating themselves for being good.

This, however, is not God's design. HE WILL NOT BLESS IT and HE DOES NOT CONDONE IT. We are to be set apart from the world. We are to look different than the world. The sheep, however, are living among the goats. God is ready to separate them.

CHAPTER 5
AND HOLY IS HIS NAME
Luke 1:49

The attributes of God are pure. Holiness is more than purity. Moral excellence cannot compare to holiness. God made us to be set apart, moral, pure, just, and truthful. For Him to be able to make us this way means that HE is MORE. More than moral, more than pure, more than just, more than truthful. We, in Christ, are capable of being all of these things. One huge difference between God and man is that He is INCAPABLE of NOT being those things.

The God of the New Testament is the God of the Old Testament. He sent Jesus to cover our faults, but God the Father cannot abide in the presence of sin at all. For God to interact with mankind He had to lower himself in the form of man. The Word of God was separated from God the Father to be able to come to a fallen mankind. The Spirit of God came upon Him to anoint and confirm Him. Through God's word (the law) and the Spirit, Jesus had fellowship with the Father as we do. Then on the Cross, he separated himself further from the Father by taking on the sins of all mankind.

God had never been separated before. Think about the lengths that He endured to be able to commune with us. It is unfathomable. This is why He deserves our most holy worship….and even then, our most holy worship is like grey to His white.

Is there anything God cannot do? Yes, amazingly so. **He cannot learn**. He knows all things, even your needs. He knows the beginning from the end. He knows when a sparrow falls. He knows every detail of His entire creation. He cannot change despite our attempts at negotiating with Him.

When we understand this, we come to Him differently. He has a design for us. It is already known to Him. Our prayers are not making God juggle His answers to determine which prayers He will answer. He has already decided. He knows His own will for our lives. Our response should be to come to Him in agreement with His will. We are to pray His will over our lives.

God knew that the Church would be in this condition. Our prayer should be that the Church line up with His will. He knows the steps that we must take to get there. He has been patient with us. Now He wants to dispense (bestow) Himself on us. We are in a season that God is going to pour out His Spirit on the Church in such a way to transform us into His design.

We are interacting with a limitless, intricate, and complicated Being. Because we are not His intellectual equal, He must communicate with us in types, shadows, stories, etc. Think about the Wright brothers going to NASA. The leadership of

NASA would have to explain to them in very simple and pragmatic steps just how they were able to build a rocket that has gone to outer space and back. It would be almost impossible for the Wrights to comprehend it. The Wright brothers could have nothing to teach NASA. However, every NASA employee would love to spend time with the Wright brothers. I can hear the brothers say, "How did they do this thing?"

The Wright brothers may understand bits and pieces of the process, but they would need years of instruction to reach that caliber. I'm convinced that most of what God tries to teach us goes right over our heads. For God to explain things to us would be like taking a tree trunk and carving it down to a toothpick so that we can hold it between our fingers. He uses word pictures, association, likenesses, etc. so that we may get a glimpse of what He is like. He is completely out of our league. We cannot handle the vastness of Him. He boils down concepts for our understanding. He uses simple language to describe incredibly complex things.

> "In the beginning God created the heavens
> and the earth." Genesis 1:1 (NIV)

This is a very simple, even childlike way to explain millions of years of creation. Physicians would explain an injury as a "compression fracture due to deterioration of a vertebrae." A four year old would say "it's broke."

If God says that your sin has been made white as snow, we can begin to understand. But if He said as white as His holiness, we would not grasp it. Association helps us to understand. However, association is not the reality...it's

LIKE the reality.

Holiness, like God's other attributes, is complex and vast. It is so serious that it creates as well as destroys. It is limitless. Yet God is attempting to give us insight into the knowledge of the holy. He is urging us to submit to it and be changed. This is the ONLY way in which we can become holy.

When Gabriel came to Mary, the mother of Jesus, to tell her that she would conceive a son (the Son of God), she said, "How can this be, since I do not know a man?" Gabriel told her, "The Holy Spirit will come upon you, and the power of the Highest will overshadow you." After Mary heard Gabriel's message she said, "Behold the maidservant of the Lord! Let it be to me according to your word." Mary was favored and beloved by God. She was a special young woman. She didn't question that God could do this miraculous thing, but she wondered how He would do it. She showed complete submission to God's will and future plans. God brought about this miracle through His Holy Spirit...all He desired was her submission and devotion. The moment her words of faith left her lips, she spoke those things that are not into existance, and Jesus was instantaneously conceived in her womb.

Elizabeth, Mary's cousin, was barren and too old to have a child, yet God opened her womb and she conceived a child, in her old age, who was John the Baptist. Just as Elizabeth confirmed Mary, John confirmed Jesus.

In the Song of Mary, she gives Blessing to the Lord for accomplishing these miraculous works:

> "My soul does magnify the Lord, And my
> spirit has rejoiced in God my Savior. For He

has regarded the lowly state of His handmaiden; for, behold, henceforth all generations shall call me blessed. For He, who is mighty has done great things; **And Holy is His name**. And His mercy is on **those who fear Him** from generation to generation. He has shown strength with His arm; He has scattered the proud in the imagination of their hearts. He has put down the mighty from their seats. And exalted them of low degree. He has filled the hungry with good things. And the rich He has sent empty away. He has helped His servant Israel, in remembrance of His mercy, As He spoke to our fathers, to Abraham, and to his seed forever." Luke 1:46-55 (KJ2000)

We, God's people, are beloved by Him. He has chosen us to accomplish His will. We must develop a personal commitment to the Lord and determine to obey God's Word; preferring His will over our own desires or fears. Mary did these things. She was abased and humble. This made her favored and loved by God.

This same posture will allow the Holy Spirit to come upon the Church, transforming it from bareness to the fruitfulness. This is God's plan. As we walk in devotion to Him, the Spirit will confirm His plan with signs and miracles.

CHAPTER 6
FOR WHATEVER THE FATHER DOES, THE
SON ALSO DOES
John 5:19

God's presence in His Church looks like something. It
doesn't necessarily look like huge numbers of people, fine
buildings, talented praise teams, or a plethora of ministry
outreaches. Respect and reverence look like something.
However, because the Church is out of synch with God, the
world questions who Jesus is, and so do most church-goers.

The religious and the God-haters will always question the
ways of God, but in this time we hear the Church questioning
"Where is our God? Why isn't He doing something about
the condition of the world?" Even the devout are weary in
faith, patience, and well doing. Their relationship with God is
strained. There is much unbelief in the contemporary church.

Jesus encountered questions from the religious and
unbelieving. In John 5, after healing the man beside the pool
of Bethesda, the Jewish leaders confronted Jesus. They
reprimanded Him for healing the man on the Sabbath. They

called it "work." The leaders continued to persecute Jesus for this. Jesus told them that He was doing what His Father was doing.

> "My Father is working until now, and I Myself am working." John 5:17 (NAS)

"Working" means the things that have been done. Jesus was telling them that the things that were done in heaven by the Father were being done by Him on earth. This sounds like the Lord's prayer: "Thy kingdom come, Thy will be done."

Luke 5 verse 18 says that the religious leaders wanted to kill Jesus for working as well as calling himself equal to God.

> "Therefore Jesus answered and was saying to them, 'Truly, truly, I tell you, the Son can do nothing by Himself, unless it is something He sees the Father doing; for whatever the Father does, these things the Son also does in like manner. For the Father loves the Son and shows Him all things that He Himself is doing; and the Father will show Him greater works than these, so that you will marvel.'"
> John 5:19-21 (NAS)

After Jesus healed the man at the pool, the man went to the Temple and told others of this miracle. Jesus found him in the temple and told him to "Sin no more, lest a worse thing come upon you". He was judging the man's condition. The religious leaders added this to their complaints. Jesus took authority over the realm of the spirits. He not only healed, but He cast out demons that had entered people through sin.

Having a relationship with the Father looks like something! It looks like the ministry of Jesus. Having a close relationship with the Father will not look religious. It may go against the grain of what is being taught and it may make some angry. One thing is for certain, a close relationship with the Father will bring life, healing, and deliverance to others.

There are churches today that don't acknowledge healing or deliverance. They don't operate in or teach the gifts of the Spirit. No wonder the Church is sick, diseased, and driven by demonic forces. Seeing a powerless Church causes many to leave the church. There are thousands in this country who profess Christ, but won't step through the doors of a church building. They hate the Church. Hurts, wounds, weariness, disappointments, and the preaching of a powerless gospel are just a few reasons. Hypocrisy is a huge deterrent for them. They see the ministry of Christ in the gospels, but they compare that to the churches today, and their hearts can't abide the lies and corruption in the church. The scriptures tell us in Matthew 24 that because of the multiplication of wickedness, the love of most will wax cold.

However, if we persevere to the end, we will be saved.

> "Once you were alienated from God and were hostile in your minds because of your evil deeds, But now He has reconciled you by Christ's physical body through death to present you holy in His sight, without blemish, and free from accusation if you continue in your faith, established and firm,

and do not move from the hope held out in
the gospel you heard, and that has been
proclaimed to every creature under heaven,
and of which I, Paul have become a servant."
Colossians 1:21-23 (NIV)

Paul told the Colossians that he was working with all of
God's energy within him so that they may know the mystery
of God. A ministry that is founded in God's Holiness looks
like something!

Although John the Baptist was considered by some to be a
wild prophet, he was called and anointed by God. He spent
time with God in the wilderness. He knew God's plan and
recognized God's moving. John had a wonderful ministry
that started in moderation and sacrifice. He was sustained
physically by little, but moved in God's power by much. He
saw hundreds repent and return to God. He prophesied
accurately to laymen and leaders. It was at the end of his
ministry that through him God reprimanded Herod. Because
of this, John was thrown into prison.

When John the Baptist was in prison he heard about the
works of Jesus, he sent two of his disciples to Jesus to ask
Him if He was the Messiah. John was anointed and preached
about the Coming of the Lord. He recognized Jesus at the
river Jordan and baptized Him, establishing Him in ministry.
John heard God's voice calling Jesus His Son and saw the
anointing of the Holy Spirit (like a dove) come onto to Jesus.
Of any person, John should have known without a doubt that
Jesus was the Messiah. John, however, did not follow Jesus
from the time of Jesus' baptism, but continued to preach
repentance of sins to the people of Israel.

As John lay in prison, he was undoubtedly weary and lost faith. He questioned his faith and the deity of Jesus. John had become offended with God because of his circumstance. John needed realignment and reassurance, so he sent two of his disciples to Jesus to ask Him if he truly is the Messiah.

The Church of God is weary. Many in the Church today are living in a spiritual prison, and/or isolated from the Church. The Church longs to know if Jesus is who He says He is, and is He the one that is coming again. By spending some time with Jesus, they can be reacquainted with Him.

John's disciples came to Jesus. Jesus tells us the same thing that he told John's men:

> "When the men were come to Him, they said, 'John the Baptist has sent us to You', saying, 'Are you He that should come? Or look we for another?' And in that same hour He cured many of their infirmities and plagues and of evil spirits; and unto many that were blind He gave sight. Then Jesus answering said unto them, 'Go and tell John the things that ye have seen and heard: how the blind see, the lame walk, the lepers are cleansed, the deaf hear, the dead are raised, the poor have the gospel preached to them. And blessed is he who shall not be offended in me.'" Luke 7:20-23 (KJ2000)

Jesus told the disciples to look at the works and make a decision as to who He was. Can the Church do that today?

Are we not to be like Him? Jesus said that the Church would do greater works than He because of His ascension to the Father. GREATER WORKS!!!! A ministry that operates in Holiness looks like something. It looks like Jesus' ministry.

No wonder the world has no need for the Church. The prince of this world already has the Church in prison, entombed, defeated, powerless, propagating dead works, and believing a lie.

Jesus explained the condition very well:

> "And Jesus went on to say, 'To what, then, can I compare the people of this generation? What are they like? They are like children sitting in the marketplace and calling out to one another', saying: 'We played the pipe for you, and you did not dance; we sang a dirge, and you did not cry.'" Luke 7:31-32 (NIV)

The people were going to God for needs, wants, hurts, and sympathy. They wanted God to intervene on their behalf without a true relationship with Him. They had no fruit of God's promises. They thought, in their self-deceived minds, that they had God all figured out and determined that He had failed them. They had made God into their own image.....and were sorely disappointed and offended.

Jesus obviously didn't fit the generation's expectation of God's answer, nor did God Himself. The people thought that they should recognize their salvation. They could not even recognize the Savior. They had no relationship with God. They had no Fear of the Lord and therefore, they had no Wisdom. They did not know Him.

"For John the Baptist came neither eating bread nor drinking wine; and you say, 'He is a demon.' The Son of Man has come eating and drinking, and you say, 'Behold, a gluttonous man, and a winebibber, a friend of tax collectors and sinners!'" Luke 7:33-34 (KJ2000)

Jesus goes on to say:

"But wisdom is justified by all her children." Luke 7:35 (KJ2000)

The Fear of the Lord is the beginning of Wisdom. Wisdom has children...byproducts. Knowledge of the Holy is understanding. Had the children of Israel had some understanding and wisdom, they would have recognized The Deliverer. How is the Church going to accomplish His Will, if we don't even recognize our Lord?

The Church has much to accomplish in these end times. We will not be able to accomplish anything without knowing our God. Abraham is called God's friend. Jesus is called His Son and we are called to be the Bride of Christ. For us to live up to our calling, we must become aware of what God is doing. We need to know His plans and directives. We need Him to be able to trust us like a friend. We need to obey like a son, and we need to be blemish-free like a bride.

It seems as though the Church has lost a lot of ground, and that it has an unattainable end. Nothing is impossible with God! God has already proclaimed our end. He has the plan, the power, and the motivation to accomplish His work in us. There is good news!

The Good news is that God is calling the Church out of the grave! He is awakening us from a long slumber. Our dissatisfaction is causing us to seek an authentic encounter with the ONE TRUE GOD, our Father, THE HOLY ONE. As we seek Him, we will repent and realign with His purposes. The Holiness of His presence will sanctify us and empower us. We will be that glorious Church without spot or wrinkle. Through His blood and spirit, we will be worthy to become partners in purpose with our bridegroom, Christ Jesus.

CHAPTER 7
OUR GOD IS A CONSUMING FIRE
Hebrews 12:29

Jesus taught us to pray that the things on earth would mirror the things in heaven. What we see in heaven is reverence for the Lord on the throne. The seraphim cover themselves and cry Holy. They have the utmost respect and are in awe of Him. This is how we must come to Him.

Although Seraphim and other angelics live in a higher dimension than we do, they are able to work in and are sometimes able to be seen in our dimension. We will ultimately live in a higher dimensional body, but we aren't there yet. Through the blood of Christ and the Spirit we are able to reach higher dimensions. On the day of His return, we will be transformed to be like Him and receive a body like His, a resurrection, glorified, 10 dimensional body. At His coming, the dead in Christ will rise first and then the believers on the earth will, in a blink of an eye, be transformed. A transition of authority will take place. For the first time since before the fall of Adam, men and women in Christ will be elevated to a higher dimension than the angels. We will be greater, just as the angels said when God created Adam.

> "It is not to angels that He has subjected the world to come, about which we are speaking. But there is a place where someone has testified: "What is man, that You are mindful of them, and a son of man, that you care for him? You made them a little lower than the angels; You crowned them with glory and honor and put everything under their feet." God left nothing that is not subject to them. Yet at present we do not see everything subject to them. But we do see Jesus, who was made a little lower than the angels for a little while, now crowned with glory and honor because he suffered death, so that by the grace of God he might taste death for everyone. In bringing many sons and daughters to glory…" Hebrews 2:5-10 (NIV)

Adam was made in the image of God, however, he (male and female) sinned and lost his standing. God sent Himself in the form of Jesus, His word made into man, to redeem mankind. Jesus was man and God. He was born into a lower standing so that He, as man, could be our high priest, offering himself as the holy and perfect sacrifice. He died and was resurrected, transformed into a higher state. He ascended to heaven as our high priest to make recompense for our sin. He sprinkled His pure blood on the mercy seat and thereby gave us entrance into heaven and into the holy of holies. He sat on the right hand of God. No longer separated from God, He returned to join the Father. He then sent His Spirit to the earth so that we, His people, could carry on His ministry. God is still with us in the form of the Holy Spirit.

Before He ascended to the Father, Jesus told His disciples to stop their evangelism, and to gather together and wait for the empowering of the Holy Spirt. As they gathered, prayed and praised God, the Spirit of God came in like a rushing wind and sat upon each of them as tongues of fire on their heads. The Spirit of God infilled them and they began to speak in other tongues, glorifying God. They went out into the streets and when the people in the city heard the tongues and the anointed preaching, they believed in Jesus.

When Jesus ascended to heaven, he said that He would come again and that He would not leave them alone. But, that He would send them the Comforter, who would teach them all things. This baptism in the Holy Spirit continues today and is not only a benefit for believers, but is still imperative if we are to gloriously finish the end of this age.

There are thousands of churches in America that reject this third person of the Godhead. Their unbelief has caused such degenerative stagnation that these churches do not look like Christ at all. They are powerless and unable to complete the task ahead of us.

The Baptism of Water is an outward manifestation of salvation. It is a physical expression of one's salvation. Whereas the baptism of the Holy Spirit is a baptism of fire, purification, and empowerment.

> "for our God is a consuming fire." Hebrews 12:29 (NIV)

When Moses spoke to God on Mount Sanai, He manifested through fire in a burning bush, but the bush was not consumed. God consumes or destroys our sin. He consumes us with His fire and we are left holy. His fire shines the light on our sins and exposes everything that is not in accordance with His will.

The Holy Spirit appeared as fire on the disciples as they were filled with His presence. This fire baptism of the Holy Spirit is He, Himself, The third person of the Godhead, in His omnipresence, coming into us. In His Holy presence we are purified, sanctified, made holy. We are changed from glory to glory. By the presence of the Holy Spirit within us, we begin to understand His mysteries. The Holy Spirit becomes our Teacher and we are changed by His Word. He is our connection to the Father. We can speak and pray in tongues directly to the Father. We can hear His voice. He will direct our paths. He can speak to others through us. We become vessels of honor for Him. His laws can then be written upon our hearts.

We who are filled to overflowing will be God's Holy fire, and become His ministers of fire. And His angels, working with us will be servants of fire and assist us in destroying God's enemies. The Holy Spirit will move through us giving signs and confirmation of God's power and authority. We will heal the sick, deliver the oppressed, loose the captives, raise the dead, open the eyes of blind, cast out demons and magnify God. He is a consuming fire, and His people will be as flames of fire. His angels will be servants of fire, and work with us to defeat God's enemies!

Who can abide the fire of the Spirit? Isaiah tells us:

"The sinners in Zion are afraid; fearfulness hath surprised the hypocrites. Who among shall dwell with the devouring fire? who among us shall dwell with the everlasting burnings: He that walketh righteously, and speaketh uprightly; he that despises the gain of oppressions, that shaketh his hands from holding bribes, that stoppeth his ears from hearing of blood, and shutteth his eyes from seeing evil; He shall dwell on high; his place of defense shall be the munitions of rocks; bread shall be given him; his water shall be sure." Isaiah 33:14-16 (KJV)

Those that can walk in His Holy fire will be the overcomers, the pure, and holy. If we allow His holy fire to burn, we will be victorious. These are the promises for those who choose holiness. He will provide the weapons of warfare and sustenance.

Righteous living is something you learn. Because of Jesus' sacrifice God helps us learn what it means to walk righteously. Through the Word, we can put righteousness on like a robe. Old Testament saints could walk in righteousness if they followed the law. However, true righteousness, the righteousness that Christ walked in, comes from the Holiness that is dispensed by the Holy Spirit. It comes from within us if we are full of His Spirit. As we repent and give God more reign in our lives we are transformed. Our thoughts and inner workings change miraculously.

Scientific researchers are studying the DNA of man and have found triggers on the DNA that effect disease and propensities for disease. Science is questioning whether these triggers can be turned on and off. They are attempting to discover if these triggers are affected by environment and genetics. God is the author of everything. Is it possible that He is able to switch these triggers on and/or off? Yes. With God, all things are possible. Is this how He manipulates our physical realm in healing or miracles? Interesting questions, however, I will leave genetic research to the scientists. One thing that is certain is that God wants to flip our switch, turn on the fire, and wake us up! This is the season that God is awakening the American Church…a church that has been sleeping too long.

The very earth groans for the awakening of the Church! Short periods of revival or refreshing are not enough. We need a reformation. Today the church in China is larger than the church in America. Healings, deliverances are happening routinely because these brethren, despite persecution, are worshipping God for who He is. God is trying to make us jealous for Him. He is calling us to become serious about His Holiness. He wants us to experience Him for who He is.

We hear of those who have died and returned, or have been caught up into other dimensions of the heavens and the one consistent thing they say is that God is Holy. Because of the revelation of His Holiness, they are changed. I don't need a near death experience to hear the Holy Spirit calling for His Church to be Holy. I hear it plain and clear. Although, I listen to the prophets today, I don't need a prophet to tell me that the Church is irreverent towards God. I see it with my eyes, and hear it with my ears. I don't need the world telling me that I am unholy, the Holy Spirit within me has conveyed that message. The point is that The Spirit and His prophets and His Church are hearing the same message from God. They bear witness with one another. And my spirit bears witness with them all.

As I preached this message, I was moved to repentance, as was my congregation. I saw my need and the need of the Church in America. I saw how much we had lost by not worshipping God for who He is. I saw how much we need in order to be risen to the standard that we are called. I saw a vision of what we will become as His refining fire is purifying us. The Church will become the Bride.

CHAPTER 8
SPOTLESS, BLAMELESS, AND AT PEACE
WITH HIM
2 Peter 3: 14

The Bride of Christ is on the way to complete
transformation. Before we are transformed into His holy
image, we must be conformed. Obviously, there is some
clean-up required. We cannot, in our own strength, sanctify
the church. However, preaching the truth about His
Holiness is certainly a key message that will unlock the
mysteries of holiness. It will effect change in the body of
Christ. Repentance, the pursuit of the things of God,
deliverance, and conformation will work together in
transforming the Church into The Spotless Bride. While
preaching the third week of the "God is Holy" series, I
experienced this very thing:

> A young woman in my church interrupted the sermon
> saying, "I don't like you very much right now". I looked
> at her with question, knowing that I had a very good
> relationship with her and found her to be congenial and

polite. She was a believer and had received the Holy Spirit with evidence of speaking in tongues. She was earnestly pursuing God. The outburst shocked me, but it took only a second to grasp what was happening. She was irritated, hyperventilating and obviously distressed. She had never exhibited behavior like this before. It was quite unlike her. Her parents were sitting next her and as my eyes went from her to her father, I knew that he was thinking the same thing... This was a demonic outburst. Thankfully I had ministered in deliverance churches and had many opportunities to cast out demons...usually by appointment or after services. I had never experienced demonic manifestation in the middle of my sermon. People usually just get up and leave the church when the demons inside of them start reacting. This woman, however, was truly seeking God. She didn't want to leave, but she did want to convey the overwhelming feelings that were happening inside of her. I remember looking at her father and saying, "Here we go." We immediately came to her and begin to cast the demon out of her. After a few minutes, the demon manifested in a piercingly loud scream and left her. She has since received more deliverance and is doing well, walking in a close relationship with God, and working in prophetic gifts, witnessing to others and telling them of her deliverance. She has an incredible desire for God and for others to know His miracle working power.

First of all, many churches today don't preach holiness. The preaching just doesn't get "hot enough" to upset demons. Secondly, the leadership would not know what to do if demons manifested in the middle of services. Most churches do not recognize demon activity and do not operate in discernment of spirits. This is interesting as it was a major part of Jesus' ministry. A great many churches believe that Christians can't have demons inside them or even be oppressed by them.

I am convinced that Christians today are walking in such oppression that it has stifled them, keeping them from walking in the freedom that Jesus paid for on the cross. Although, I am attempting to write about the Holiness of God, it is impossible to not mention the antithesis to that holiness. The reason that the Church looks like the world is that the Church is not free from the love of the world and demonic influence.

Over and over Christians ask for forgiveness of their sin. God does forgive them. If we study God's word, over time, we will be able to completely walk in that freedom. If demons cannot manifest, they will move on to another victim. However, for those Christians who find themselves in a revolving door, committing the same sin over and over, deliverance is a wonderful benefit of the gospel of Christ.

Experiencing God's Holiness exposes the demonic realm. The Holy Spirit within us shines light on the darkness that is inside of us. This is God's intention. He is Light and there is NO darkness that can stand up to Him. My message series on God's Holiness sparked a weekly home meeting in which I taught on deliverance. People were set free from demonic activity. God's presence was confirmed with many signs. I saw people change before my eyes. My congregation has new hunger for the things of God, a new desire for more fellowship, and a deeper love for each other. They are full of faith to see what God will do next.

Seeing this has brought so much life to our congregation. It has blessed me. But more importantly, we are seeing God for who He is. We are not ashamed of looking foolish because we are seeing repentance, deliverance, salvation, and healing. The captives are being set free. We are experiencing His Holiness and His Goodness.

While preaching this message, we shut down most of the praise practice (for a season) in order to spend time with God in corporate prayer, worship, expressing our fear and reverence of the Lord. I have changed the way that I view God and the way in which I come to Him. I have changed the way that I think and act toward others. It seems that I have started running every thought through God's Holiness filter, weighing and dividing everything by His Holiness. I am being transformed.

When we are aware of His Holiness, we are held to a higher standard. When we continually walk in His Holiness, we can be trusted by God to follow His command, reach out to His creation, and touch His people. So many people have been hurt by the Church. That was not and is not God's fault. It is our fault and He wants it to stop. He wants us to care for them as He does. As we walk in His Holiness it causes us to desire His Heart. His Heart is full of love. As we experience His Heart, we will love others as He does, without judgement or condemnation. Holiness prompts us to speak the truth with love and lead others in a right relationship with Him.

The pressure on today's American Church to be "successful" is overwhelming and not God inspired. It's fleshly and demonically driven. God's barometer of success is completely different from ours. God wants submission, not success. He wants worship and honor, not numbers and busy-ness. God wants us on our faces before Him, in His word, hearing His voice, following His strategy.

It is interesting that Jesus, a carpenter, did not spend any time constructing church buildings. However, He followed God's design accurately and completely. He spent time with His Father. In the presence of God, our motivations, plans, and hopes will come into proper alignment. As we gain the Fear of the Lord, our ministries will look different.

The Church has lost a lot since the days of the early believers. We are recognizing that our status quo is not working. The standard that the Church is setting has been too low, and the standard of self-promotion must come down. God is not blessing our dead works, He never did. Pastors are burning out and falling as they try to maintain a success that God did not perform.

We must hold God's Standard up for the world to see. Spending time with Him will open the heavens so that His direction can be known. We, like the Israelites, must be led by God. If we want victory, God must be in our midst. When God was living with the Israelites, the Ark of the Covenant went before them. His presence, His Shekinah, gave them light. Shekinah means the dwelling place of Him Who dwells.

When the tabernacle was built, God's Shekinah was in the Holy of Holies. His Glory was an amazing thing. People, who acted outside of God's design, died in the presence of this Holiness. His Glory was and is an awful and terrible thing to be feared. The priests prepared themselves by sacrifice and ritual before entering His presence. A rope was tied on the priest's ankle so that if the high priest died in God's presence, the other priests could pull him out. We must take God's Holiness seriously.

The atoning blood of the sacrifice, reverence, and obedience allowed the high priest into God's Holy presence. Why should it be any different today?

Think of Paul on the road to Damascus. He was full of pride, religion, and hatred of Jesus' followers. When God's Shekinah Glory appeared to Paul, it blinded him (It could have just as easily killed him). And God said, "Why are you persecuting me?" Paul fell to the ground. There is just no arguing with God's presence. It demands a change in attitude and posture. God's presence brings us face to face with our sin. It shines the light on everything that is not God. God had to show Paul that he, in all his intellect and fervor for God, was truly blind and an enemy of God. How many today would be knocked to our knees when confronted with His Holy Glory? All of us!

His Spirit, this consuming fire, is being poured onto the earth. The hot coals, like a waterfall, are being poured out. You can dabble at the edge of the pool and receive a little, or you can get into the force of the waterfall and be cleansed, fully baptized in His Spirit, and prepared for service. The last manifestation of this fire will be the judgement that God pours out on ungodly men.

"By the same word the present heavens and earth are reserved for fire, being kept for the day of judgment and destruction of the ungodly. But do not forget this one thing, dear friends: With the Lord, a day is like a thousand years, and a thousand years are like a day. The Lord is not slow in keeping his promise, as some understand slowness. Instead, He is patient with you, not wanting anyone to perish, but everyone to come to repentance. But the day of the Lord will come like a thief. The heavens will disappear with a roar; the elements will be destroyed by fire, and the earth and everything done in it will be laid bare. Since everything will be destroyed in this way, what kind of people ought you to be? You ought to live holy and godly lives as you look forward to the day of God and speed its coming. That day will bring about the destruction of the heavens by fire, and the elements will melt in the heat. But in keeping with his promise we are looking forward to a new heaven and a new earth, where righteousness dwells. So then, dear friends, since you are looking forward to this, make every effort to be found spotless, blameless, and at peace with Him." 2 Peter 3:7-14 (NIV)

God is calling for repentance and holiness. All things will be consumed by His fire…starting with us and ending in the complete destruction of the heavens and the earth. We are coming to the end of this age and a new age is on the horizon.

> "...You, Lord, in the beginning laid the
> foundation of the earth, and the heavens are
> the work of your hands. They will perish, but
> you remain; they will all wear out like a
> garment; You will roll them up like a robe;
> like a garment they will be changed. But you
> remain the same, and your years will never
> end." Hebrews 1:10-12 (NIV)

The fabric of space will wear out. Like a robe God will remove it. Space will be folded in on itself. Einstein said that all space is not just emptiness, but has matter in it. Space is like a fabric, it bends on itself. The earth was placed on this fabric, bending it. The moon rotates around the earth further bending the fabric of space. Science shakes hands with scripture. More and more, Science is confirming God's word.

One theory says that space is expanding. Others say that Einstein may not have been correct about the consistency of light. If that is true, let's say that there was a big bang and light exploded and was fast, but now is slowing down. The Hubble telescope has shown stars outside of our universe that are dying off. Which means that it is possible that Hebrews 1:12 has begun. Could it be that the next age has already begun and will be ready in 1000 years? Are we now part of a contracting universe as God rolls it up like a garment? The ways of God are often times incomprehensible to the natural mind. God allows all creation to have its completion and he will roll it all up like a robe, then He will create a new heaven and a new earth. We, His holy and righteous children, will inhabit the new creation.

I say all of these things to help you understand the complexity and holiness of the God we serve. He is Creator, Destroyer, and Judge. He is awesome and awful. He is glorious and terribly holy.

How is it that we think that we can dictate to God how things must be? He is going to roll up all of creation and we stand on the earth as an ant raising our fist to Him, dictating our demands. We dissect His Holy word and only ingest those parts that please us. We ignore Him at our convenience. We are one heartbeat away from eternity and we think that we can manipulate the one who upholds everything? We dare to come to Him in that kind of posture.

> "Are you not from everlasting O Lord my God, my Holy One? We shall not die. O Lord, you have ordained them for judgement; and, O mighty God, you have ordained them for correction. You are of purer eyes to behold evil, and cannot look upon iniquity: why then do you look upon them that deal treacherously and hold your tongue when the wicked devours the man that is more righteous than he?" Habakkuk 1:12-13 (KJ2000)

Don't we ask these questions of God frequently? The answer is that He is incredibly long suffering. His wish is that everyone repent, be saved, worship Him, and live with Him. His Great Love is as complex as the heavens and their creations.

"Consider also that Our Lord's longsuffering brings salvation, just as our beloved brother Paul also wrote you with the wisdom God gave him. He writes this way in all his letters, speaking in them about such matters. Some parts of his letters are hard to understand, which ignorant and unstable people distort, as they do the rest of the Scriptures, to their own destruction. Therefore, beloved, since you already know these things, be on your guard not to be carried away by the error of the lawless and fall from your secure standing." 2 Peter 3:15-17 (BSB)

He gives others every opportunity to repent. However, when the cup of iniquity is full, God will arise and judge the wrong doers, the sinners, and the wicked. There is an appointed time for His judgement. We are living in the final days before this judgement. God is arising!

As a child, we can all relate to instances when we were doing something that we shouldn't be doing. Daddy tells us to stop it. We hear, but continue in our mischief. He might tell us again, but we continue. However, when Father's long suffering is over and he stands up, we know that we are in trouble. If we haven't stopped what we were doing by that point, reprimand and discipline are on the way! When God arises, His enemies, and ours, will be scattered! When God's people arise, the devil with be smacked down!

In Ezekiel 1 we see the angelics in heaven ministering with fiery coals. The movement of their wings sound like the rush of many waters. They responded to the voice of the Almighty and it sounded like the noise of an army. Ezekiel says that the vision described the likeness of Glory of the Lord.

The fire is being poured out upon us. The Water Gate is opening and the Waters are beginning to rush. God is pouring out a new move upon the earth, the likes of which the earth has never seen. The Church needs to step into the fire, wade into the waterfall. As we obey, we will then be transformed. His Voice is being heard and His army is being prepared. We will storm the gates of hell, loose the captives, and perform the greater works that Jesus spoke of. We will walk in all that He has spoken and we will be His glorious church and all will see His Glory.

CHAPTER 9
THE KIND OF WORSHIPPERS THE FATHER
SEEKS
John 4: 23

Our first response to God must be WORSHIP. Do not come to Him with needs, wants, or desires.

> "Yet a time is coming and has now come when the true worshippers will worship the Father in spirit and in truth, for they are the kind of worshippers the Father seeks. God is spirit, and his worshippers must worship in spirit and truth." John 4:23-24 (NIV)

If you think that you are a worshipper, but you spend no time in devotion to Him, you are self-deceived. If you minister to others in His name, but you do not know Him, you misrepresent the standing you have with God. A dead relationship leads to dead works.

Jesus saw this in His people and preached against it. He explained it to a Samaritan woman at Jacob's well in Sychar.

The Samaritans were not supposed to talk to the Jews. A woman was not to speak with a man without her husband present. Rabbis had no business speaking to shady women. But Jesus saw her real thirst and changed their conversation from the natural to the spiritual, offering her salvation.

> "Jesus answered, 'If you knew the gift of God and who it is that asks you for a drink, you would have asked Him, and He would have given you living water.' 'Sir', the woman replied, 'You have nothing to draw with and the well is deep. Where can you get this living water? Are you greater than our father Jacob, who gave us the well and drank from it himself, as did also his sons and his livestock?' Jesus said to her, 'Everyone who drinks this water will be thirsty again, but whoever drinks the water I give them will never thirst. Indeed, the water I give them will become in them a spring of water welling up to eternal life'. The woman said to Him, 'Sir, give me this water so that I will not get thirsty and have to keep coming here to draw water.'"
> John 4:10-15 (NIV)

She was only concerned about her needs. She didn't understand what he was saying, but, she was interested.

> "Jesus told her, 'Go, call your husband and come back.' 'I have no husband', she replied. Jesus said to her, 'You are right when you say you have no husband. The fact is that, you have had five husbands, and the man you now

have is not your husband. What you have just said is quite true.' 'Sir', the woman said, 'I can see that you are a prophet. Our ancestors worshipped on this mountain, but you Jews claim that the place where one must worship is in Jerusalem.'" John 4:16-20 (NIV)

When confronted with her sinful fornication, she deflects the conversation away from her sin. Isn't that what we sinners do? When feeling convicted about our sin, don't we deflect, trying to hide it, steering the conversation off of our problems?

"Believe Me, woman, Jesus replied, 'a time is coming when you will worship the Father neither on this mountain nor in Jerusalem. You worship what you do not know; we worship what we do know, for salvation is from the Jews. But a time is coming and has now come when the true worshippers will worship the Father in spirit and in truth, for the Father is seeking such as these to worship Him. God is Spirit, and His worshippers must worship Him in spirit and in truth.' The woman said, 'I know that Messiah (called Christ) is coming. When He comes, He will explain everything to us.' Jesus answered, 'I who speak to you am He.'" John 4:21-26 (BSB)

When we come to God with a heart that wants to understand, He will have answers for us and He will reveal His purposes.

Jesus' disciples returned and saw that He had been speaking to the woman and they asked why He had been talking to her. She left. She left her clay jar at the well and went into town and said to the people

> "Come, see a man who told me everything I ever did. Could this be the Messiah?" John 4:29 (NIV)

The people of the town came to Jesus because of her testimony. The disciples had bread from the town and urged Jesus to stop and eat first.

> "But He told them, 'I have food to eat that you know nothing about.' So the disciples asked one another, 'Could someone have brought Him food?' Jesus explained, 'My food is to do the will of Him who sent me and to finish His work.' Do you not say, 'There are still four months until the harvest?' I tell you, lift up your eyes and look at the fields, for they are ripe for harvest. Already the reaper draws his wages and gathers a crop for eternal life, so that the sower and the reaper may rejoice together." John 4:32 (BSB)

Jesus saw that she was ready to be harvested. She forgot all about being thirsty, left her jar and went into town to tell the people about Him. His disciples were concerned about physical needs. They could not see God's bigger picture. The woman's sin had been confronted, she realized that the dead works people were arguing about had produced nothing but continued thirst. She sought understanding. She looked for the Messiah. Her posture changed at the well. She went from thinking fleshly to spiritually in one interaction with the Messiah.

Because of her, Jesus stayed in Sychar two days and many more believed because He could see the spiritual readiness of the people. He was in perfect alignment with the Father and did not miss the opportunity to bring salvation to many in that town. He wasn't afraid to break man-made rules to get to her. He broke religious ideology to bring her truth. He revealed Himself to her.

God wants us to know that if we align properly with Him, we will move beyond flesh and fear. How many of us have held back? God has given us ideas, unctions, and leadings, but because of fear, we are paralyzed and do not have faith in Him. God desires that we grow close to Him as a Bride. The love of a bride for her new husband is perfect. Perfect Love casts out fear. On the wedding day, a bride should be fully confident that she is loved.

> "If anyone acknowledges that Jesus is the
> Son of God, God lives in them and they in
> God. And so we know and rely on the love
> God has for us. God is love. Whoever lives
> in love lives in God, and God in them. This
> is how love is made complete among us so
> that we will have confidence on the day of
> judgement: In this world we are like Jesus.
> There is no fear in love. But perfect love
> drives out fear, because fear has to do with
> punishment. The one who fears is not made
> perfect in love. We love because He first

loved us. Whoever claims to love God yet
hates a brother or sister is a liar. For
whoever does not love their brother or
sister, whom they have seen, cannot love
God, whom they have not seen. And He
has given us this command: Anyone who
loves God must also love their brother and
sister." 1 John 4:15-21 (NIV)

As the husband cares for his wife, faith grows. When we are
close to Him, we will have faith in Him, fearing nothing.
Worshiping God, for who He is, will draw us into that type of
relationship. Intimacy with God is absolutely necessary for
this type of intimate intercourse. It is God intertwining with
His people in which there is inability to discern one from the
other. We need to blur the lines of His Person and our
person. For a bride to give herself to her husband, and the
husband to the wife, there must be openness, humility, faith,
and love.

Out of a desire, the newlyweds look for ways to please each
other. We look for ways to please God and as we do, our life
will change. He blesses us abundantly, so expect Him to fulfil
His promises as you seek Him.

I am convinced that by His Blood, and His Spirit, it **is**
possible to walk in holiness. I'm not talking about
performing religious or legalistic acts. I'm talking about
appropriating His holiness in our lives. God is Sovereign and
He is the originator of holiness. As we must respond
appropriately to that sovereignty with reverence and faith, we
can be His holy people.

"Make every effort to live in peace with everyone and to be holy; without holiness, no one will see the Lord. See to it that no one falls short of the grace of God and that no bitter root grows up to cause trouble and defile many." Hebrews 12:14 (NIV)

Your bitter roots defile others! Kick them out of your garden. If you harbor unforgiveness, FORGIVE. You must forgive others if you want the Lord's forgiveness. Without forgiveness, there can be no holiness.

Family curses can be stopped with you. Generational curses can be broken. I have seen it. He wrote your DNA, He can change it! If the enemy attacks you, say NO! If you have a disease, God can heal. If you are afraid, spending time in God's word and in His presence will give you faith. If you are weak, find your strength in Him. THERE ARE NO EXCUSES. GOD HAS THE ANSWER TO EVERY PROBLEM IN YOUR LIFE. Don't make excuses for your shadow sides, REPENT!

Pray with me:

> Heavenly Father, King Jesus, and Holy Spirt, how GREAT You are. I worship You for who You are. I come to you in fear and reverence because You are Holy beyond my thoughts. You are Almighty in power, and Your mercy is more than I can contain. Your loving kindness flows over me like a warm oil and causes a sweetness to permeate my being. Your blood is pure and I am covered in Your

holy sacrifice. You have proven Yourself to
be more than worthy of my respect, praise,
and adoration. I do adore You, Lord. I praise
You. I give You honor and blessing. I bless
your name....That name that is above all
names. You are God alone. You are high and
lifted up. There is no other like You. Self-
existent, Glorified, and Omnipresent God, I
love you. I thank You for all of Your
attributes. You are perfect in all Your ways.
You are Light and there is no shadow of
turning away from those You love. You are
the potter, I am the clay. You are my Father,
and I am Your child. You are my King, I will
obey. You are my Lord, the love of my life.

In Your presence, Oh Lord, I see my iniquity and sin.
I confess these sins to You:
_____. Forgive me for not
putting You first, for not seeking You first, and for
not worshipping You as I ought. Forgive me for
getting caught up in things that don't matter. God, I
am convicted and led to put You first in all things. I
have faith in You. I place You First. Your kingdom
and Your plans come first. I pray and agree that
Your kingdom would be manifest on the earth
through me and all of your people. I seek a greater
life with You. Blur the lines of my life and Your
presence. I have no idea what will happen, Lord, but
I trust in You and know that I will be changed.
Conform me to Your image. Show me the plans that
You have for me. As I place You in the proper place

in my life, show me how to love You more. Holy
Spirit, fill me with Your fire. Baptize me in Your
Presence. In the name of Your Son, Jesus, Amen.

Start seeing the trials in your life through His eyes. They are a
tool to strengthen you, to establish you in your faith. Trials
give you an opportunity to seek Him more, standing firm on
the hope of your victory. The angelic host is fighting on your
behalf! God hears your prayers and His military forces
(angels) are working on your victory. Daniel experienced this
after he saw a great vision. He was on his face before God.
He could not understand the vision. He became tired of
seeking God for the answer, but suddenly an angel appeared
to him:

> "Then behold, a hand touched me and set me
> trembling on my hands and knees. He said to
> me, 'O, Daniel, man of high esteem,
> understand the words that I am about to tell
> you and stand upright, for I have now been
> sent to you.' And when he had spoken this
> word to me, I stood up trembling. Then he
> said to me, 'Daniel, for from the first day that
> **you set your heart on understanding this
> and on humbling yourself** before your God,
> your words were heard, and I have come in
> response to your words. But the prince of the
> kingdom of Persia was withstanding me for
> twenty one days; then behold, Michael, one of
> the chief princes, came to help me, for I had
> been left there with the kings of Persia. Now

I have come to give you an understanding of
what will happen to your people in the latter
days, for the vision pertains to the days yet
future"' Daniel 10: 10-14 (NAS 1977)

Although some answers come immediately, others do not. It
took 21 days of battle for the message of God to get through
to Daniel. God, however had dispatched the angel on the
first day of Daniel's prayer. Be steadfast in your faith! God
is sending help! He will get the answer to you.

Set God's bar high in your life. Pursue holiness. Raise His
banner for your entire family, and the world to see. God has
the answer to the world's problem. There is no lack in His
kingdom. His governments are perfect. No one is ill, all are
cared for. **May His kingdom come on earth as it is in
heaven!**

Worshipping and communion with God will give us a
"kingdom mentality". Our needs and wants disappear as His
desires and purposes come into focus. We begin to see
ourselves as a partner….a **partner in purpose** with Him.

"Truly I tell you, whatever you bind on earth
is bound in heaven, and whatever you loose
on earth will be loosed in heaven. Again, truly
I tell you that if two of you on earth agree
about anything you ask for, it will be done for
you by my Father in heaven. For where two
or three come together in my name, there am
I with them." Matthew 18:18-20 (NIV)

We have used this scripture when praying for things that we
think we need. Looking at the context of this scripture, it

was spoken by Jesus to instruct His disciples in proper judgement of someone who is apostate. Then Jesus goes on to speak of forgiveness and unforgiveness. Judgement is a Holy thing and we need to take this seriously. There is a time to come together and judge the works of a man, whether they be in error and repentant or be rebellious and need discipline. Judgement is not given to children, but to mature, holy ones of God. We are supposed to execute His judgement righteously. As the Church is purified, it will not only be able to forgive the sins of man (dispensing God's forgiveness), but to judge the workings of Satan.

This is a higher calling for the Church. Let's get our eyes on Him! Let's get our eyes off of our own needs and desires. Let's be about our Father's business.

Chapter 10
BUT THE EYES OF THE LORD ARE ON
THOSE WHO FEAR HIM
Psalms 33:18

If you take God lightly, you won't experience God. However, if you take God and His Holiness seriously, you will experience God Himself. There are great benefits in taking His Holiness seriously.

> "But the eyes of the Lord are on those who
> fear Him, on those whose hope is in his
> unfailing love, to deliver them from death and
> keep them alive in famine. We wait in hope
> for the Lord; He is our help and our shield.
> In Him our hearts rejoice, for we trust in His
> Holy name. May your unfailing love rest
> upon us. O Lord, even as we put our hope in
> You." Psalms 33:18 (NIV)

His eyes are on those who FEAR Him.

He loves us enough that He wants us to know who He is. In this, He will protect us against our enemies and our own failings. God looks upon us in such compassion and love that He wants to provide victory in our lives. Like any good father, we have a spiritual Father who is beyond good, and is willing to bless us as we obey.

The world may look hopeless, but God sees something entirely different. He sees every knee bowed, and hears every tongue confessing Jesus as Lord. The God that we approach and preach must be the Everlasting, Awful, Holy God who has pure eyes that will not behold evil and will not look upon iniquity. "Technically saved" Christians who confess salvation but have no other fruit in their lives demonstrate a compromised lifestyle that is unable to stand in His presence. All Christians are being convicted by his Spirit of Holiness to allow His transforming power to change them. God never changes...We must change. He sees His people as an extension of His grace and goodness, proclaimers of His Holy Standard, preachers of the Gospel of Christ, Warriors for His Kingdom, Sons of thunder, and ministers of fire.

He sees a Glorious Church without spot or blemish. Circumstances do not define God's Truth! His Word will accomplish EVERTHING that it is supposed to accomplish. There is no problem too great for our God. There is no government that can stand against Him. He is our protection. He is our deliverer. No weapon formed against His people will prosper for they carry His purpose, His power, and His banner! His people will dispense His love, order, and His judgement.

No one can modify God or His requirements, and His requirements are high. Those that do not meet them will not see Him. There is already a victor in this battle of the ages.

Satan is defeated and Christ is exalted in all the earth. The battle has already been won! We are to execute His orders and judgement. We are to dispense His Grace and Mercy. We are to be as white as snow, covered in His blood, walking in His Love and working by His Spirit. We are coming into the finest hour of the Church. We will shine, for His Light Has Come! His Angels are pouring out from heaven **all provision** necessary to finish this age. As the Church submits to Him, His transformation power is at work. While preaching this message I saw His power at work:

> An entire family was delivered and healed. This family of 4 (father, mother, teenage son, and 21 year old daughter) were all diagnosed with depression, anxiety, and/or mood disorders. They were all on antidepressants. The son took antianxiety medication as well. The daughter, diagnosed with bipolar disease, was on both an antidepressant and a mood stabilizer. Two of them were under the care of a Psychiatrist. During this message, they repented and began pursuing God in a deeper way. Demons were cast out, healing was received. They each believed that God had healed them. Two of them weaned off of their medication over a couple of months. The daughter who suffered with bipolar disease went completely off her medication (cold turkey). This family of four was completely healed. There was no pressure applied by myself, my parishioners, or from each other. They all believed that God had

delivered them and they acted on it. To this day, several months later, they are free and remain off medication. No longer bipolar, the daughter believes that it was a demon that was cast out that was causing the disease. She said that she knew when the demon left her that she was healed. There has been no sign of disease or episodes since.

The father and mother of this family said that the only thing that is different off the medication is that they now have more feelings of empathy and compassion towards others. The father stated that the medication had numbed him and that it had been a very long time since he really cared about anything. He now feels compassion for others and is able to love others like he hadn't for years.

The Holiness of God led an entire family to repent and receive freedom and healing. How GREAT IS OUR GOD? HE IS BEYOND GREAT!

I don't know the specifics about how God does these miraculous things. He may change us at the cellular level. What I do know is that it was a miracle for this family and it has brought them closer to God. It is a monument for me to look back on and know that God is Great!

I am in no way saying to go off your medications. I didn't tell them to do that, and I won't ever tell anyone to do that. If God heals you, you will know it. You can discuss it with your doctor. God's miracle power will stand up in the court of medical science. I have to tell you that the mother of this family is a critical care nurse with many years of experience. She did not take these decisions lightly, especially the decisions her children made.

Depression is one of the most common illnesses in America and affects over 16 million adults each year. (www.mentalhealthamerica.net) Statistics cited on this website are staggering. After many years of ministry and counseling, as well as my own bout with depression, I believe this is a true reflection of Americans today. Medicine treats the symptoms, but the medical community has not found the cure. This family found the cure in God. I am convinced that God alone is the cure. Americans, even Christian Americans, are plagued with the results of living a life outside of God's design. Whether it be depression or any other disease process, a right relationship with God is the medicine that everyone needs.   If the medication is numbing people so that they cannot feel God's love or conviction, then they certainly could be easily led away from God.

When I think of all the Christians that are needlessly suffering in the area of their mind, I am saddened and moved to intercession for them. I know that it is not God's design. We see many times in which Jesus cast out evil spirits. Many today could be free if the Church was walking in the holiness that Jesus walked in and of which He ministered.

> "They sailed to the region of the Gerasenes, across the lake from Galilee. When Jesus stepped ashore, He was met by a demon-possessed man from the town. For a long time this man had not worn clothes or lived in

a house, but he lived in the tombs. When he saw Jesus, he cried out and fell at His feet, shouting at the top of his voice, 'What do You want with me, Jesus, Son of the Most High God? I beg you not to torture me!' For Jesus had commanded the unclean spirit to come out of the man. Many times it had seized him, and though he was chained hand and foot and kept under gaurd, he had broken his chains and been driven by the demon into solitary places. Jesus asked, 'What is your name?' 'Legion', he replied, because many demons had gone into him. And they begged Jesus not to order them to go into the abyss. A large herd of pigs was feeding there on the hillside. The demons begged Jesus to let them go into the pigs, and He gave them permission. When the demons came out of the man, they went into the pigs, and the herd rushed down the steep bank into the lake and was drowned. When those tending the pigs saw what had happened, they ran off and reported this in the town and countryside, and the people went out to see what had happened. When they came to Jesus and found the man from whom the demons had gone out, sitting at Jesus' feet, dressed and in his right mind, and they were afraid. Those who had seen it told the people how the demon-possessed man had been cured. Then all the people of the region of the Gerasenes asked Jesus to leave them, because they were overcome with fear. So He got into the boat and left. The man from whom the demons had gone out begged to go with Him. But He sent him away, saying 'Return home and tell how much God has done for you.' So the man went away and told all over the town how much Jesus had done for him." Luke 8:26-39 (NIV)

There is so much revelation in the account of this incredible deliverance. Jesus went across the sea from Galilee to Gerasenes for one encounter that would reach an entire town. The area was filled with wealthy people who raised and sold pigs (an unclean animal that the Israelites were not to eat). What a sight it must have been to come upon this crazed human being living in the tombs. He was naked and dirty. At some point he had been chained, but had broken through the chains and was terrorizing the community and blocking the entrance into the city. When Jesus approached, the demons inside of the man knew exactly who Jesus was and what He was capable of. Interestingly, they knew their final destination as they asked Him not to cast him into the abyss. It wasn't time for the abyss. However, the abyss is coming for Satan and his hoard legion.

Jesus gave the man a quicker release by allowing the demons to go into the pigs, which the city valued more than God. Can you imagine the miracle that took place? The herders and owners of the pigs were undoubtedly upset about the loss of their income. The owners of the pigs came out of the city to see what had happened. They asked Jesus to leave! They didn't care about the man's freedom or deliverance (they had at some point chained him up). There was no love in them.

The freed man begged to go with Jesus, but he was instructed and released into evangelism of that very town. By removing the blockade of the city (the demoniac), more evangelism could occur. The Church grew in that area until the 600's AD when Muslims invaded. The town today is named Kursi which means "throne" or "stronghold". Could this city have been the throne of the satanic prince that ruled over it? This city was important to our God. God will lead us to go places and talk to people who are important in His strategy.

I can't help but think of the multitude of mental hospitals filled with suffering people. Without sedation, they too, would be naked and restrained. This is not God's design. The love of God in us compels us to cast out demons and set the captives free.

God's miraculous power flowing through us is a promise for those who fear Him. It comes through repentance and relationship. His Word, mixed with faith, and the power of His Spirit are no match for disease. God is higher than disease. Name any disease, and His Name is higher! The name of Jesus is above every name. You are in Him and He is in you. Simple math tells us that if that is so, we are also above disease. The key is being **in Him**. Filled to overflowing with His Spirit, His Love and compassion. We can no longer hold back God's love from the world, for if we do, we are no better than the citizens of Kursi.

CHAPTER 11
LET US FIX OUR EYES ON JESUS
Hebrews 12: 2

There is no doubt that God is waking His people up and a new move has begun. What will this new move look like? It will look like **Repentance, Reconciliation, Restoration and Reformation**! It looks like the Father, the Son, and the Holy Spirit. It looks like heaven's kingdom coming to the earth. It looks like the Sons of God manifest. It looks like the rebuilding of His governments in the church. It looks like the worship of heaven and the robes of righteousness. It looks like the totality of God moving through His people.

On October 31, 1517, almost 500 years ago, God began the restoration of His truths to the church. Martin Luther, a monk and theologian, nailed his theses on the door of the Catholic Church in Wittenberg, Germany. He protested the indulgences of the Roman Catholic Church. With that "scornful" action, The Protestant Reformation was poured out on the world. Luther taught that salvation was through the Grace of God, not works, and could not be bought. This truth seems so obvious today, but it was heresy at that time, (much like preaching deliverance from demons is heresy today in some churches). Luther brought many life altering changes to believers. Since that time, God has restored truths to the Church in increments.

All of the moves of God brought an attribute of God to light. They brought restoration of a truth that had been stripped from the Church. With all the moves since the 1890's to 2016, none have brought the totality of God. The "Pentecostal or Holiness movement" in the late 1890's started with authentic devotion and the infilling of the Holy Spirit, but ended in legalism and false humility. The "Fundamentalist Evangelical movement" 1920's brought great salvation and stood against the sins of society. Their crusades saw thousands come into the body of Christ, but the lack of teaching about the things of God propagated a weak Church. In the 1940-50's, great healing ministries with authentic results occurred, but were not sustained by most of the leadership. The lack of personal integrity was the demise of some. The "Charismatic movement" of the 1950-60's came in and broke the legalism that the evangelicals were walking in. They preached about the Holy Spirit and saw healings, deliverance, and miracles. Bibles schools and conventions were overflowing with people. For some, the move ended in lasciviousness. The 1960's brought the "Jesus movement" in which people could come to Jesus just as they were. Non-denominational churches sprang up all over. They taught only the milk of the word and created a weak and anemic Church. The "Faith and Teaching movement" of the 1970's-1980's brought God's people the divine truth of the authority of the believer, however, people became off balanced and used their faith to "get what they lusted after" from God. The "Prophetic movement" came on the scene in the 1990's. Hearing the voice of God was magnified in the Church. This brought direction to God's people, however, some gifted but greedy men fell into temptation. False prophets arose and some in the Church were deceived. There were people all over the country who would not seek God for themselves, but repeatedly sought out a word of prophecy for their lives. The rejection of the prophets led to isolation of some, and left them subject to deceiving spirits. This move is still present and those that have stayed in fellowship and closeness to God are hearing God and declaring the things that I am preaching and writing about. Today, the "Apostolic movement" is in infancy. Although, it started off a little shaky with self-appointed Apostles popping up out of nowhere, we are beginning to see God's appointed Apostles. They are now coming on the scene to help restore Church doctrine, empower the Church to walk in its rightful purpose, and prepare or "equip" the saints for the harvest that is soon to come.

All of the previous moves originated with God. He was depositing parts of Himself into His people. These moves restored a piece of God's character and strategy. They all restored aspects of the 5-fold ministry offices. God will always send Himself to reach His people. When God moves on the earth, great things happen (until the enemy gets in somewhere). This does not shake me. God knew exactly what would happen. He was not surprised. He is our All Knowing God. He had a plan and it went exactly as planned. He is in control of all His strategy. Our part is to stay in Him, stay in fellowship, to rightly divide the instruction received from the Spirit and confirm it through His Word and Offices of the 5 fold ministry.

We must not be paralyzed from the mistakes of the past but learn from the old and proceed. Don't despise small beginnings. Glean the truth, forgive the fallen, and move on with God. In every movement, there were great workings of God and failures of men. The Christians that fell away were following the wrong thing. They were following men, leaders in the various movements. When the power to heal subsided, some followers left. When faith didn't bring the desire of some people, they left. When a minister fell due to sin, some followers left. Those that left and turned away from God did not know God. They were following the cloud, but didn't know the God in the cloud. They will not inherit His Kingdom. I did not say that they weren't saved. That is up to God. I don't judge them. I have been hurt in church as well, and realize the temptation to abandon God. However, I know my God. He never fails or disappoints. If I am disappointed, it's a sign that I must realign myself with Him.

God is going to resurrect all the truths from those movements. He is raising up his Apostles who will insist on balance, depth, and holiness. They will facilitate His army. They will join the seasoned Prophets who are hearing from God and decreeing God's purpose. The Evangelists will be VERY busy in the fields of harvest, for it is ripe once again. The Pastors and Teachers will lead, guide, instruct, and disciple this influx of believers. All of these offices will work in concert and unity to accomplish ALL OF HIS PURPOSES. **THESE ARE THE DAYS OF RESTORATION!**

The Gifts of the Spirit are being restored to the church. As we walk in His Spirit and His character, the fruits of the Spirit, we will see God's hand move mountains, shake nations, loose the captives, give sight to the blind and raise the dead. God is ARISING and His Church is preparing themselves, coming to attention, and seeking their marching orders.

There are those, even the very young in the Lord who will walk in such holiness, justice, and power that some weak Christians will be become jealous. Those who are mature must rise up to guard and protect the young from destruction for they have been given a double measure of God's Spirit for this time. They are motivated by purpose. They are seers and oracles. They may appear as John did in the wilderness. They are not able to be tamed by the world. They belong to God. They may be perceived to act restlessly because they will be like Jehu who drove like a wild man to kill God's enemy, Jezebel. What they lack in wisdom, they earn in zeal. That is why they will need the partnership and wisdom of those seasoned in the ways of God.

When you see God's plan in the Spirt, it is easier to believe when it come to pass in the natural. When God's miracles are seen, the youth of this nation will know that the very thing they have been seeking is God. The youth of this nation are hurting, and fed up with the hypocrisy that they have seen. As they come to God, they will be set afire. The mature in the Lord must let the new generation in God be free, but provide an anchor and support to them. The wealth of knowledge that the older saints have gleaned over the years will culminate in a glorious move of the Lord.

There are people living today that have not experienced a true outpouring of God. They are not jaded. They, like the Samaritan woman, are seekers of truth and spirit...just the people God is looking for in this time.

The population of my congregation is, for the most part, seniors. I believe that God is going to move on His people over 50 in such a way that has never been seen. The young and the old working together to accomplish His will. There are so many seniors that have experienced God's miracle working power of the 40's-60's and they saw it pass away. Those that have not fallen away are in the wings yearning, praying, and waiting for the waters to be stirred again. Jesus is saying "rise up and walk". There are thousands of them traveling in their motor homes, living their retirement for themselves. But God is calling them into service! They have the resources and the time to invest. They just need a reason, a purpose. They need to see God's hand. As God calls them to repentance and holiness a renewed vigor, hope and faith will come. They will live a long life motivated by wanting to see the return of the Lord. When we mix this maturity and availability with the health and stamina of the youth, we have a winning combination.

We must realign our hearts to His purpose. Most manufactures of vehicles suggest that the wheels should be realigned every 5,000 miles. Proper wheel alignment plays a huge role in you driving from point A to point B. Alignment effects fuel efficiency, tire wear, tire performance, vehicle handling, and maneuverability. Wheel alignment is a big factor in a vehicle's steering response. If you are going on a long trip, you want to align the wheels before the trip starts so that you don't run off the road or have to stop in the middle of your journey. Being in correct alignment with God will keep you on the right path. The Church has come a long way and has a few more miles to travel.

As we come to end of this age, all things are speeding up. God is redeeming the time. What used to take 10 years may take 2. The time is short and things in God are about to explode. You won't want to miss a thing! The old saints would have loved to have lived in our time. Their prayers are with us. We should feel some responsibility to them as well as to Jesus to finish our course in victory. The saints in heaven are watching us, cheering us on. They are excited for this time.

> "Therefore, since we also are surrounded by such a great cloud of witnesses, let us throw off every encumbrance and the sin that so easily entangles, and let us run with endurance the race set out for us, fixing our eyes on Jesus, the author and perfecter of faith, who for the joy set before Him endured the cross, dispising its shame, and has sat down at the right hand of the throne of God." Hebrews 12:1-2 (NAS)

Embracing His Holiness is so important for us to be able to travel with Him. We must set aside every weight, every sin that holds us back. We must seek a close relationship with our God, the Father, the Son, and the Holy Spirit. Jesus is the author and finisher of our faith and our holiness. Through Him we are saved and in Him we are meant to walk in holiness.

"Consider Him who endured such hostility from sinners, so that you will not grow weary and lose heart. In your struggle against sin, you have not yet resisted to the point of shedding blood. And you have forgotten the exhortation that addresses you as sons: 'My son, do not make light of the Lord's discipline, or lose heart when He rebukes you. For the Lord disciplines the one He loves, and He chastises everyone He receives as a son.' Endure suffering as discipline; God is treating you as sons. For what son is not disciplined by his father? If you do not experience discipline, then you are illegitimate children and not true sons. Furthermore, we have all had earthly fathers who disciplined us, and we respected them. Should we not much more submit to the Father of our spirits and live? Our fathers disciplined us for a short time as they thought best, but God disciplines us for our good, **so that we may share in His holiness.** No discipline seems enjoyable at the time, but painful. Later on, however, it yields a peaceful harvest of righteousness to those who have been trained by it. Therefore strengthen your limp hands and weak knees. **Make straight paths for your feet, so that the lame will not be debilitated, but rather healed. Pursue peace with all men, as well as holiness, without which no one will see the Lord."** Hebrews 12:3-14 (BSB)

CHAPTER 12
FAITH WITHOUT ACTION IS USELESS
James 2:20

Faith and holiness go hand in hand. They are absolutely necessary for us to move forward. We must participate with God in accomplishing His will. Participation means "work". We are foolish if we think that we don't have to use faith to make decisions, take chances, move forward, take risks, and invest energy, time and resources. Faith without works is dead. And the opposite can be said. Faith is a powerful action step, but Faith without holiness can cause us to be haughty and unloving.

> "What good is it my brothers and sisters if someone claims to have faith but has no deeds? Can such faith save them? Suppose a brother or a sister is without clothes and daily food. If one of you says to them, 'Go in peace; keep warm and well fed,' but does nothing about their physical needs, what good is it? In the same way, faith by itself if it is not accompanied of action, is dead. But someone will say 'You have faith, I have deeds.' Show

me your faith without deeds and I will show
you my faith by my deeds. You believe that
there is one God, Good! Even the demons
believe that and shudder. You foolish person,
do you want evidence that faith without deeds
is dead, useless?" James 2:14-20 (NIV)

Our actions must reflect God. Jesus did what He saw the
Father doing. He walked in Holiness and **acted** by faith. He
was **busy** about His Father's business. This sounds like
work; action; busy.

All mankind has been given a "measure" of faith. God wants
us to grow in faith by studying His word, His actions. By
prayer and application of His truths, we grow in faith. If we
set up monuments (all the things that God has done for us) in
our hearts and memories, we can return to that monument.
This will increase our faith to believe what He will do next.
Spending time in devotion will give you boldness to use the
faith that you have. Consult Him, make a decision and plan
of action, invest in that choice and watch what God will do.
Go through His testing with faith that He will come through
for you. After your success, you can revisit this victory over
and over as you give thanks to Him. Your faith grows like a
seed. Plant it and see God's mighty hand.

Walking in faith is a decision. It is a choice that must be
tested. A boat that is not tested in a storm, may sink. That is
why all products that are made must endure rigorous tests of
many types. The purpose is to see if the product will stand
up to any environmental stresses. Boats, jets, and military
equipment must go through extraordinary testing, because
failure means casualties. God doesn't want casualties in his

body or His creation. He must test us so that we will stand up when it really matters. David was tested with the lion and the bear before taking on Goliath. In contemplating Goliath's threat, David remembered his monument of defeating the lion and defeating the bear. He saw that Goliath was not circumcised and had no covenant with God. David remembered the covenant God had made with Israel. His faith grew and when it mattered, David killed the giant and saved his people. David showed his faith by his works.

Action steps is another word for WORK. When you truly know God, there is a joy that comes with doing His will. When He can trust you, He can show you mysteries that are hidden; His plan of attack…strategy. Just as David saw the five stones and knew what to do, you will know. David used only one stone to kill Goliath, but he had an action plan in place in case he needed to confront Goliath's 4 brothers.

Working with God will bring joy and satisfaction. Step out and do the things that His spirit leads you to do. Show Him that you believe and trust Him. Unless you do these things, you won't see the full gospel manifested in your life. Living by faith is not comfortable and requires you to enter into a place in which you are unfamiliar, but the scripture tells us that the Justified Ones will live by faith.

In this world that wants to drag every human being down into the abyss of sin, it is a great challenge for any believer to walk in holiness, righteousness, and faith. However, if you don't apply yourself, you won't receive God's full blessing. Like faith, true holiness cannot be acquired without action steps. Determine that you are going to cooperate with God in transformation. Surrender and show Him that you are serious about your repentance. Expect and allow Him to change you. When His Spirit urges you to resist sin, resist. When He leads you to do something, use your faith and do it.

You can be delivered, you can resist temptation. Depression, fear, addictions to pornography, gluttony, lying, stealing, and disease have been put under your feet. Use Action steps to take your freedom. With God's Holiness working, you will be free. We are in a war until the war is done. Say 'No' to sin and resist the enemy. Whatever your struggle, God knows and wants to deliver you. If you have tried your best to resist, but you feel driven and stuck in a revolving door of sin and repentance, seek deliverance. More than likely you are dealing with a demonic spirit that is inside of you, driving you. Thankfully, we don't have to do this in our own strength. His Holiness is Powerful. Seek ministry from those that have experience and can instruct you. If you are involved in a church that does not believe in or operate in deliverance, find one that does. If you go to a church that charges money for God's free gift, leave and find a church that is walking in "free-dom."

We fight a spiritual battle. Our weapons are spiritual. We must strive to fight against the sins of the flesh, sins of the eyes and the pride of life. Just saying that God will cover our sin is not enough. Jesus did cover our sin and we are forgiven when we repent. However, many times Jesus said, "Go, and sin no more." We must step out of the rut of old patterns. Many times it takes change in our lifestyle or friends. We have to change the patterns of our mind. If we feed on sugar, we will want more sugar, but if we feed on God, we will want a closer relationship with Him.

If you want God to be very interested in you….Fear Him. Psalms 18:33 says that His eyes are on those who fear Him. Seek Him. Evaluate your motivations, actions, and thoughts frequently. Realign yourself to His purpose and His attributes. Focus on His Holiness and repent when you are convicted. Don't resist repentance. When you remain in sin, you open the door to demonic activity in your life, you lose boldness with God, and your heart begins to harden as you justify your sin. God responds to your rebellion with discipline, because He is a good Father.

Sheep are obedient. Goats are rebellious. Right now, the goats and the sheep live together. However, God's Holiness is separating His sheep (His people) from the goats (all those who do not fear or know Him). Ask yourself which side you are on. You will have to walk in holiness to stand for God. Your walk of holiness will be tested because God has a future plan. He is not just thinking of this age, but He is strategizing for the next. I believe that He is preparing us for the new millennium. Between now and the Millennial Reign, there is a very important heavenly event to take place. The Marriage of the Lamb to the Bride and the great Mercy Seat Judgement will happen before the one thousand year reign of Christ on the earth.

> "So we make it our goal to please Him,
> whether we are here in this body or away
> from it. For we must all appear before the
> judgement seat of Christ that each of us may
> receive what is due us for the things done
> **while in the body**, whether good or bad.
> Since then, we know what it is to fear the
> Lord, we try to persuade others. What we are

is plain to God, and I hope it is plain to your conscious." 2 Corinthians 5:9-11 (NIV)

"It is written: 'As surely as I live, says the Lord, every knee will bow before me; every tongue will acknowledge God.'" So then, each of us will give an account of ourselves to God." Romans 14:11-12 (NIV)

This judgement is for all saints who have lived the Church age. It has nothing to do with our salvation and entrance to heaven. What will happen is that we will stand before the Lord and our life will be placed in the purifying fire. Our dead works will burn like chaff. Whatever remains will be like golden crowns awarded to us. We will then take those crowns, the things that we have done at His command, (the remnants of our life) however small or large, and present them to Our Lord, crowning Him with many crowns.

I think there will be jewels in the crowns of those that have walked in His Spirit, His Holiness and obedience to His commands. I want many crowns with many jewels, to give to the One who saved me from the fiery pit. Jesus has done so much for me. Because of the thanks and gratefulness that I feel, I don't want to stand before him at that ceremony with nothing to give Him. I hope you feel the same.

How sad we will feel if all that is left on the altar is ash. Our sin and indifference will not endure the fire. Excuses for not serving Him fully will not endure the fire. Nothing outside of Holiness will endure the fire.

God's people will achieve holiness by **His** Power. He is moving to complete the work he began in us. **In truth, His**

Body, His Church is already holy. The Church is just experiencing an identity crisis of sorts. God made it known that there are certain things are holy…set apart for Him: The Name of God, human life, marriage, sexual intercourse, the sabbath , the tithe, and those that are His…the Church. Peter said we are a chosen people, and royal priesthood and a holy nation! (1Pet 2:9) We are holy because He has set us apart and indwells us.

We must see ourselves as holy. Our identity is a holy one, set apart, consecrated to Him. He is restoring all things, and He will restore our identity of holiness.

> "…because of your partnership in the gospel
> from the first day until now, being confident
> of this, that He who began a good work in
> you will carry it on to completion until the day
> of Christ Jesus." Philippians 1:5-7 (NIV)

Join me in this prayer:

I worship You My Father. You are Holy and Worthy. I fear You and reverence You. I choose to surrender to You and Your Holiness, knowing that You are working in me that I may show the good, acceptable, and perfect will of God in my life. I choose to lay aside every sin that takes me away from Your presence. I humble myself before You and ask that You align me to Your will. Show me the shadow areas of my soul that need Your Holy cleansing. Lord, you knew that I would meet you at this time on this day to reveal Your Holiness to me. Thank you for including me in Your plans and purposes. As I am tested, help me to prove that I can be trusted with the keys of your kingdom. Show me what part I

am to play in bringing this kingdom to those around me.
Show me the things that I am to do in Your Name that I may
have many crowns to lay at Your feet. You alone are worthy.
In the Majestic Name of Jesus, Amen.

REFERENCES:

NAS: New American Standard Bible, (first published 1963, complete bible published 1971

http://www.abarim-publications.com/Meaning/YHWH.html#.WRsh0vnyupo)

NIV: New International Version Bible, (first published 1978, revised 1984, 2011)

AKJV: American Kings James Version Bible, (put into publication in 1999)

KJ2000: King James 2000 Bible, (finished in 1993)

ESV: English Standard Version Bible, (originally published 2008)

KJV: King James Version of Holy Bible, (originally published 1611)

BSB: Berean Study Bible, (published 2016)

NAS1977: New American Standard Bible, (published 1977)

http://www.metalhealthamerica.com

ABOUT THE AUTHORS

Peter Balciunas has been serving in the ministry just shy of 30 years. His journey has allowed him the privilege of participating in almost every area of ministry from youth pastoring, leading worship, church planting, and apostolic leadership. Peter and his wife, Patricia of 23 years have 2 lovely children, Chandler and Laurel. Peter loves sailing, music, photography and cinematography. Ten years ago, Peter founded and remains pastor of Awake Christian Church in Melbourne, Florida. He has a passion to help people to awaken to their true God-given identity as he leads the charge to set God's people free while shining light on the truth of who our God is. One truth that resonates with Peter is that God is HOLY.

Alison Bitney is a wife, mother, registered nurse, teacher, and author. She and her husband, Brian, have been married for over 35 years. She and Brian were in the ministry in the 1980's and pastored a church in California. They strayed from God and lost almost everything. Alison has a beautiful testimony of how God restored her dignity, marriage, relationship with her family, and her finances. She and her entire family are now members of Awake Christian Church, where they found an accepting environment for repentance and restoration. She has 2 children, Andrea and Grayson Bitney. Alison resides in Melbourne Florida where she serves as a prophetic intercessor. She longs to see people set free from spiritual and emotional torment, while her work as a critical care nurse gives her many opportunities to share the love of Christ with those who are physically ill.

Made in the USA
Columbia, SC
07 January 2025

49770318R00061